Destiny, Purpose and Calling

Copyright

Dedication

This Book is dedicated to the friends of God.

May you find your life's purpose hidden deeply in His heart.

Acknowledgements

Thank you to God for the inspiration and orchestration of this unexpected book. This project has been a gift from Father, Lord Jesus, and Holy Spirit from beginning to end and I trust it will encourage kingdom purpose, calling, and fulfilment of destiny for each one who reads it.

I thank my family: Bob my dear husband of 41 years, who has lovingly encouraged me in my callings throughout our years together. Thank you to our children Ben, Kyle & Katie, Rachel & Jamie, Abby & Dan, and Caleb. Watching each of you rise up into your callings and purpose has inspired me as a mother to offer this small work in the hopes it will mentor others.

Thank you to my proof reading, test driving friends: Karin Trory, and Catherine Self, who have helped to work through the glitches with much joy.

To my editor Rachel Arsenault, huge thanks for your labour of love, your passion for the subject, and professional handling of this material.

I sincerely thank John King for his work and teaching on the Manifestational Gifts. Your work for our King is truly inspirational and an example of a man living in God's purpose.

Thank you to my son Caleb and his many friends in the Ottawa Christian DJ community, as well as all those who were part of our fellowship group there. Thank you to the women at the Dundas/Ancaster soaking group as well as the Peterborough Women in Prayer group. Your journeys have seeded the genesis of this book.

Contents

Action Steps

Suggestions for Use

This book is designed as a working guide to clarify your God given purpose, to assist you in discerning your calling, and to ultimately enable you to live in the fullness of your God given destiny. You may be at any stage in life: just beginning to think about direction; transitioning from one phase to another; in the midst of raising a family or career and wondering how this phase fits into your destiny; or wondering about the legacy you will leave your descendants.

As you go through this book I suggest you go slowly no more than one chapter per day. Even though you could read through this book in much shorter time you will receive the most benefit as you work slowly and prayerfully doing the exercises.

The Life Plan Action Steps are designed to bring clarity and focus. They will help you discern where you have come from, where you are now, and where you are going along your journey into God's good plans for you. The action steps at the end of Chapter 8 will help to move you into the next step of your journey.

Many people find the practice of listening prayer or soaking and meditation brings much deeper revelation of God's perspective, so the book is designed to incorporate these practices. As you work through each chapter take the opportunity to ponder and soak in each concept. Then journal your questions and God's response in the pages provided so that you may re-read what has been discovered in the months and years ahead. It is so encouraging to look back and see how God has fulfilled His promises, plans and brought you into a fresh perspective on your life[1].

---

1   See "Listening Prayer" Appendix 1

For Group Use:

1. The group could read each section together or before you gather.

2. The group could practice listening prayer together, asking the provided questions.

3. After recording individual insights you could share together the revelation Holy Spirit has unveiled to each one.

4. The group may then like to pray for one another; that God will bring further revelation, that He will empower, and give grace to fulfill His desires through your life.

I pray you will use this book as a launching pad to bring clarity and enlightenment to the pathway God has for your future. May you connect with God in a deeper way as you grow in your knowledge and love of Jesus Christ.

Love and Blessings, Rev. Yvonne Prentice

Chapter 1: The Books of Destiny

I want to share a metaphor with you that God gave me several years ago. It has helped me to understand God's perspective on destiny. During a time of pondering the subject I had a visual experience of going with Jesus into a heavenly library. We went into a room where I was shown books of destiny. There were completed books on one side, so many volumes one could not possibly count them, but what really caught my attention were the books of destiny in progress, mine was among them. Jesus took my book off the shelf; what I saw surprised me. It was not a book as we would recognize one; it did not have any pages but was in the form of a movable sand art picture. At first I didn't understand how it could be my destiny but Jesus explained it. As I go through life and make choices the frame tilts, the sand shifts and forms differently making the "sand-scape" change. God's plan for my destiny is the solid frame, it remains constant, illustrating that destiny is fixed but how it formulates is ever changing based upon how I choose to live. There is a perfect formulation or rhythm of life that God would prefer for me but that is dependent upon whether I choose to live in agreement, and close connection with Him. The choice is mine: the life of union and overcoming grace found in God or life lived my own self- centered way determining my own path based on selfish choices. One way builds God's Kingdom with joy and freedom, the other fulfills my destiny but at loss to me. Depending on how selfish my choice I could possibly even bring loss to the Kingdom of God.

The vision I experienced brought clarity to me, as well as noting the many illustrations in Scripture of destiny lived out in victory and defeat. Following are some Biblical examples from destinies now completed.

Samson the Reluctant Deliverer

Let's first take a look at the life of Samson, recorded in Judges 13 to 16. In his life story we read Samson is the Judge of Israel for 20 years. We will probably all agree that Samson does not live out his destiny in victory, though he does accomplish what God predestined him to do, despite his issues. Samson never really accepts the Nazirite calling or his vocation as a Judge of Israel. Samson's life ends in slavery, he has no descendants. Let's examine what blocks him from fulfilling his destiny in victory and honour.

- Samson's parents receive an angelic visitation and strict instructions for his upbringing. At the end of the chapter we read that the Lord blesses him as he grows and the Spirit of the Lord begins to take hold of him. However, in chapter 14 Samson notices a Philistine woman and demands his parents arrange marriage to her, even though his parents strenuously object. While it is not God's preference that he rebel, Samson's attitude shifts the circumstances around him, which create "Plan B" so to speak. God then creates an opportunity to disrupt the Philistines oppressive hold on the Israelites using Samson's rebellious nature.

- Samson does not value the gift of strength or the Nazirite calling which is evident when he defiles himself by eating honey from a dead lion's carcass. He even dishonours his parents by giving some to them without disclosing the unclean source from which the honey came.

- Samson does not value his heritage as an Israelite but desires to have Philistine women. This is in violation of God's laws as well as another example of not honouring his parent's advice.

- Though God does amazing feats through him and for him, Samson does not value his relationship with God as special. He insists on his selfish desires and on exacting revenge, which ends in utter humiliation for Samson. Even so God's plan is not thwarted, the Philistines are defeated, and their leadership put to death[2].

Joseph the Victorious Journey

In Genesis 31 to 45 we read the story of a young man born into his father's favour, who suffers at the hands of his envious brothers. Joseph lives a difficult but overcoming life of continuous humility and submission to God. Joseph, the favoured son, is sold into slavery because of jealousy. The favour of God on his life allows him to do so well in Potiphar's home that he becomes its manager, until the blow of false accusation lands him in prison. In prison Joseph receives favour due to his character and God's providence and is given managerial privileges. Finally, by God's design Joseph is positioned to advise Pharaoh and became second in command of the most powerful nation in the region. He finishes his life fulfilling His destiny in a place of victory and honour. We see throughout his life that Joseph has a deep trust that God would fulfill the dreams He had given. Joseph also displays a grasp of the larger purposes of God that are being worked through each difficulty. Joseph's family life also prospers. At the age of 30, he is given a woman of influence (Asenath) for his wife. He has two sons whose names are a testimony to his victory over adversity. He calls them, Manasseh meaning, "God has made me forget all my troubles and the family of my father", and Ephraim meaning, "God has made me fruitful in this land of my suffering"[3].

Joseph begins with a lack of discernment (at best) or a prideful attitude (at worst) in announcing his God given dreams to

---

2   Judges 15: 18-20

3   Smith, William, "The New Smith's Bible Dictionary" Edited by Reul G. Lemmons in Association with Virtus Gideon, Robert F. Gribble, J. W. Roberts. Garden City, New York: Doubleday & Company Inc. 1966.

his family. This provokes jealousy among his brothers, and he quite quickly feels the consequences of his mistake in announcing his God given dreams. It seems the humiliating circumstances do not cause him to be embittered or to give up. He makes the best of the difficult circumstances and is able to walk in favour throughout the trials he encounters.

- He values the dreams God gave and hangs onto them until fulfillment.
- He gives honour to God as the one who gives both dreams and interpretations.
- He is a man of prayer and discernment, using wisdom and growing in each vocation.
- He understands the timing of God and learns to discern the character of others before trusting them.

Joseph credits God with working the things the enemy meant for evil into good, thus avoiding bitterness anger or discouragement.

In contrast with Samson, Joseph receives an inheritance to pass on to his descendants. The legacy Joseph's descendants are allotted is a double portion of land when Israel enters the Promised Land.

When we compare the lives of Samson and Joseph we note there was no family line after Samson but Joseph's family benefits for generations to come from his faithful and obedient attitude. Other examples of lives which show destiny and calling follow. You may find it interesting and helpful to read their stories and learn more: Abraham & Sarah, in contrast to Ananias & Saphira, Moses in contrast with Ahab, Deborah in contrast with Jezebel, David in contrast with Solomon, Paul versus Ananias, the high priest in Israel, as well as many others. The most perfect example of a destiny fulfilled is that of Jesus himself. Our Lord lived the amazing life of humility and obedience which changed the world forever. His life is the only example of destiny lived out in perfect union with God's design.

We see from these lives that God`s purposes and will for our destiny will come to pass, however how this happens depends upon our yieldedness and our relationship with Him.

Before we go any further into the exploration of this topic I feel it necessary to include dictionary definitions of the words "destiny", "purpose", and "calling". I found it very helpful in understanding and perhaps you will too.

Definition of Terms:

Destiny

The fate to which a person is destined, the preordained or predetermined ordering of events, the power that is thought to predetermine the course of events.

Purpose

Something to be attained, a thing intended, the reason for which something is made or done, to have one's purpose; design or intent. Doing something on purpose or intentionally.

Calling

Convocation or summons, a vocation or profession, an inwardly felt call or summons to an occupation.

These terms play-out in lives very specifically. Consider the lives of Samson and Joseph, which we briefly explored earlier in this book. Below I have laid out how the concepts of destiny, purpose, and calling applied in their lives to bring clarity. Keep in mind the full understanding of these concepts will be explained in detail as the book continues.

The Example of Samson

It was Samson's destiny to put an end to the Philistine leadership that had dominated and preyed upon Israel. Samson was called as a Nazirite to be a Judge over Israel. This calling, or occupation, required a strict life-style, one that would have brought a disciplined example to the Israeli nation and preserved their society to be an example to the pagan nations around them. Instead he disregarded his calling and lived as the pagan nations, bringing dishonour to himself and perverting the course of his destiny. Samson's purpose was to glorify God and make him known among the nations of his day by liberating God's people from the Philistines.

The Example of Joseph

It was Joseph's destiny to preserve Israel through drought and famine. He was called to manage household affairs in his parental home, then in the household of Potiphar, after which his prison term served to expand his skills into the management of an institution. The earlier callings or occupations of Joseph served to prepare him for the eventual position of governing the national affairs in Egypt. His purpose was to glorify God and make Him known among the nations of his day by leading in the preservation and deliverance of God's people. This he did through his leadership position in Egypt during the time of famine.

We can look back over the life of a person like the Apostle Paul and see that he was destined to be the apostle who brought the kingdom truth of Jesus Christ the Messiah to both the Jewish and Gentile people groups of his day. Paul wrote much of the New Testament letters, encouraging the people of God to follow the truth and persevere in the faith and in righteousness. Paul's purpose: to know God and make Him known, wherever he travelled, was pursued with much passion. Through several phases of life, both as a Jewish Pharisee and Christian apostle, tent maker and even prisoner, Paul worked passionately in each calling.

My Legacy

Write your own Eulogy: If you were attending your own funeral what would you like said about you?

What kind of person do I want to be remembered as?

_____

_____

What things do I want to be remembered as having accomplished?

_____

_____

What legacy do I want to leave to the future generations?

_____

_____

What Kingdom legacy or accomplishment would I most want to be remembered for?

_____

_____

You may wish to pray about your desires and ask God to align your soul to His perfect desire for you. Following is a sample prayer to help you.

Dedication Prayer:

Father God, thank you that my life has been designed by you for a purpose with a wonderful destiny in mind. I choose today to align myself with your plan for my life. Lord I want to please You by fulfilling the destiny You have assigned to me with

honour, glorifying You in the process, and fulfilling
Your kingdom purpose. Lord Jesus I thank you
for your resurrection power that enables me to
accomplish everything you have set before me to
do. By following your example Jesus I purpose by
Your power to live in union with You by Your Spirit.
Holy Spirit search me and show me what good
gifts You have put in me to motivate, and enable
me to increase the Kingdom of Heaven here on
earth. In the name of Father, Son, and Holy Spirit.

I purpose by the power of the Holy Spirit to discern
and follow your plan and purpose for my life.
Father I choose your will above my own today
and fully rely upon Your power to perform my
calling and complete my destiny. Thank You for the
purpose You have given me in this life to know You
and make You known. May I live in your purpose
and respond to your promptings and direction for
life. In the name of Jesus Christ, Amen.

Chapter 2: Created for Purpose

God had a wonderful purpose in creating mankind. We see it in Genesis on the sixth day of creation God said,

> *"Let us make people in our image, to be like*
> *ourselves. They will be masters over all life...*
> *So God created people in His own image; God*
> *patterned them after Himself; male and female*
> *He created them God blessed them and told*
> *them, multiply and fill the earth and subdue it.*
> *Be masters over the fish and birds and all the*
> *animals." (Genesis 1:26–28)*

The Garden Experience

God created us with capacities like His own so we could receive His love and companionship. He gave work to Adam and Eve immediately; that of tending the garden He had made to sustain them. This work was not labour intensive before the fall; all they had to do was pick what they needed to eat. However, they were to master, occupy, and keep this garden. God gave them work to give meaning and form to their lives. With God's authority, they were to keep watch over the garden, to tend it and keep it in order[4]. The word "keep" is translated from the Hebrew word *shamar* which means to guard or protect. So, Mankind was given meaningful work to do, tending and watching over the earth, which gave a sense of purpose to them. Work brings meaning to life but often the true purpose of our existence is veiled to us. Our work, though it can be motivating and satisfying, is not the sole purpose for which we

---

4   Genesis 2: 15

were created. A big clue as to the reason and purpose for our creation is revealed by the way God chose to be most noticeably present in the Genesis of mankind's first days.

God enjoyed the cool of each day with the family He created, walking together with Adam and Eve in the Garden of Eden. Their communication was unhindered. God's presence was most keenly noticeable to the first people as they had this pleasant time, after their work, enjoying Him. Man finds satisfaction and meaning in work but God's pleasure is to be with us. He delights in giving us purpose through work, however His true joy is in sharing His thoughts, companionship, and in communicating His love to us. God's desire to create living beings capable of receiving His love, with the capacity to enjoy His company, was fulfilled in Adam and Eve. God's purpose for creating us was not that we do work for Him, but that we will enjoy being with Him. That we will be recipients of His love and love Him in return. I believe God desires we have even greater fellowship with Him than Adam and Eve first had with Him. He desires us to live in constant communion or union with Him.

God In My Garden

It was God's passion to reinstate and enhance the friendship and communication lost at the tree of the knowledge of good and evil. His great sacrifice, (the death, burial, resurrection, and ascension of Jesus Christ) made possible the reinstatement of the communion once experienced in the garden. He made this life of friendship contingent on the will of each person choosing to receive His offer of forgiveness and cleansing. The choice to be near Him is ours but we must come on His terms. This means receiving forgiveness and reinstatement as God's children through the blood payment of Jesus Christ. We do not have to pay the price, but we do have to turn back to Him in connection and communication with Him. It is His design that we take hold of our purpose and turn our attention toward Him. This is putting the gospel of Jesus Christ in simple terms.

What Jesus did is much deeper that the few words I have just written. As I mentioned, I feel God's desire for unhindered communion (common union)[5] goes further than merely restoring us to the level of friendship the original dwellers of the garden had. God's passion is that we live in union with Him through the Holy Spirit every moment of the day not just at the end of the workday. That God would be in the garden of our spirit and soul is in fact one of the main reasons Jesus Christ gave up His life. His act of sacrifice paid not only for original sin (the disobedience of Adam and Eve) and personal sin (our own acts of disobedience), but dealt a deathblow to the sin nature, which has kept each of us from friendship with God. This garden of communion (or Eden) is now open to us 24/7 as a continuous spirit to Spirit connection with God.

So dear reader, here we are in our time in history, how do we now pursue our purpose? I believe purpose is not hiding but being unveiled. Every person is given original purpose: to live with God in unhindered relationship as sons and daughters. As we do this we will reflect the likeness of our Creator. Some have put purpose more simply: To Know God and make Him known. This is also reinforced and taken a step further by the answer Jesus gave the Pharisees as to which was the greatest commandment.

> Jesus said, "Love the Lord your God with all your heart, all your soul, and all your mind. This is the first and greatest commandment. A second is equally important: Love your neighbour as yourself. All the other commandments and all the commands of the prophets are based on these two commandments" (Matthew 22:37–40)

Jesus includes in His answer the degree to which God would have us know Him...to love God with our entire being and then also to make God's love know to your neighbours by loving

---

5   Definition of common: meaning together or belonging to all. Definition of union: oneness, the act of joining two and forming a compound body

them as we would want to be loved.

Purpose on Purpose

This broad purpose, for all mankind, is then carried by each one of us through our individual lives. At the heart of every human being our core purpose is to love God and radiate His life and likeness. Only by coming into agreement with that core purpose will we find fulfilment. Our individualized interpretation of the fundamental reason for existence could play out something like the examples below:

- A creative artistic person may use their talent (art, writing, drama, craftsmanship) to first seek God's inspiration through communing with Him and then illustrate their love of God, (as well as God's love for people) creatively through their art.

- A businessperson works their business in such a way to include God's input and principals of practice for the good of their employees, customers and community as opposed to profiteering. His or her close friendship with God would give birth to innovative business ideas, which would enrich and enlarge their influence in the world around them.

- A parent would listen to God for the way each child needs to be loved and directed; parenting from God's voice, exemplifying to the child a life lived in union with Jesus and imparting that lifestyle to the next generation.

- In interpersonal relationships as we live out of our original purpose we will prioritize our friendship with God. As we do this our souls are satisfied and full because we live in communion with Him. We will not be looking to our friends to meet our need for love and acceptance, but rather, from our full relationship with God we will be able to love others and give to them, and enjoy healthy relationships.

We see in these examples lives based on the fundamental purpose for human design, operating for the betterment of individuals and the community to which they belong. In friendship with God the deepest needs of our soul are satisfied. The amazing thing is that as we fulfill our purpose to love and fellowship with God, His deepest longing is met also. God desires our companionship, love, and attention. He is not in need of these, however, He desires that we turn to Him to receive His fullness. As we do He enjoys being with us, as well as communicating His love and desires for our lives.

It is not hard for us to understand God's desire. Any parent or grandparent relates to this kind of longing or desire. How blessed and pleased we are when our children, especially adult children, come to us for no other reason than to enjoy being together with us. As they share their hearts, we listen and share ours. The mutual enjoyment is very precious; we look forward to these kinds of visits when our children do not come because of obligation, or because they need something, but from the pure love of being together. This is how our Father feels about us.

Purpose is not what we must search or work for; purpose is unveiled internally in our souls through the process of communion with God. In the process of growing in our friendship with God, our personal identity unfolds; our purpose is manifested and shaped through our lives. As we live in union with Jesus Christ, through Holy Spirit, in the abiding presence of Father God, we find the answer to why we are here. Purpose is found in connecting with the heart of God.

Listening Prayer

Have some time listening or soaking to hear God's response to these questions about purpose[6]: For Example:

Lord Jesus how is my greater purpose (to love you and make your love known to others) walked out in my life?

_____

_____

_____

_____

Or ask Holy Spirit please speak to me about how You want Your purpose to be lived through my life.

_____

_____

_____

_____

---

6   For how to practice listening or soaking prayer see Appendix 1

Chapter 3: Kingdom Calling

*And so dear brothers and sisters, I plead with you
to give your bodies to God. Let them be a living
and holy sacrifice – the kind He will accept. When
you think of what He has done for you, is this
too much to ask? Don't copy the behaviour and
customs of this world, but let God transform you
into a new person by changing the way you think.
Then you will know what God wants you to do and
you will know how good and pleasing and perfect
His will really is. As God's messenger, I give each
of you this warning: Be honest in your estimate
of yourselves, measuring your value by how much
faith God has given you. (Romans 12:1–3)*

The Scripture above gives some directives, warnings, and
promises on the topic of understanding and living in God's will.
The words apply to our calling in a very tangible way. If we
want to know what God wants us to do with our lives both for
earthly accomplishment and eternal kingdom gain. If we are to
know how good, pleasing and perfect His will really is, we must
comply with things Apostle Paul has laid out.

Give Your Bodies To God as a Living Sacrifice That He Will Accept

The kind of sacrifice God accepted in the temple was the
lifeblood of a holy (set apart), clean (not a designated unclean
animal) offering, which was dedicated to God by the priests.
In the same attitude God wants us to give ourselves (Spirit,
Soul and Body) as a living sacrifice. Not to die and give up
life, but to live, dedicated to fulfilling His plans. In order to do

this we need to give Him our spiritual allegiance completely, having no other gods beside Him. We must dedicate to Him the faculties of our souls[7] so they will be Holy (set apart, clean, and acceptable) for His use. We must surrender our gifts, talents, and possessions to God, who gave them all to us originally, so He can renew our thinking and use of them. Finally, we must give up our ambitions for the future in favour of His calling.

Don't Copy the Behaviour and Customs of This World

Though we are in the world we are, in actual fact, citizens of Heaven[8]. The culture of Heaven is radically different than that of the earth and our lives need to emulate Heaven's ways. So we need to take our queues from God, not from the culture around us. This takes a realigning of our perspective so we can yield to God's work and ways within us.

Let God Transform You By Changing the Way You Think

By choosing to focus on God, submitting to His promptings and yielding our souls to Him, God will transform us. God will change the way we think so that our desires and passions will be in line with His will.

Be Honest In Your Estimate of Yourselves

We are children of the Most High God so to underestimate ourselves is not honest. If we only take into account our own abilities, or inabilities, we leave God's power out of the equation. Conversely to decide to take up a career without knowing if it is God's plan for us is overstepping our bounds (without God we can do nothing)[9]. Either end of the spectrum; whether we under estimate our abilities in God or take our

---

7   By faculties of the soul I mean the mind, will, emotions, imagination, and conscience
8   Ephesians 2: 19-22, Philippians 3: 20-21
9   John 15: 5

future into our own hands without consulting Him, is not being honest in our estimate of what we can accomplish together with God[10].

Measure Your Value By How Much Faith God Has Given You

Faith is given by God as we draw upon Him. Everything accomplished through God's power is done using faith (acting before we are sure of the result). If we step out in faith, not knowing the results but trusting in His power, with regard to calling, God will empower all He has called us to accomplish.

Lifetime Calling?

Most of us believe the decisions we make around our profession or occupation will have a crucial effect on how our lives play out. Many people get stuck in indecision for years as they try to decide which direction they need to go with education or time and financial investment in business etc. Often the tendency to procrastinate or hesitate over our future career is due to the belief that we are about to set our lives on a permanent track. Some common concerns are:

- That we may choose a career we will eventually hate or that leaves us living in mediocrity, both in our income and job satisfaction.
- We may choose an occupation we will fail at, losing time, money, and self-worth in the process.
- Our vocation will be meaningless with no lasting impact.
- That we could choose a job that is not God's choice for us and that we would have to repent and begin all over again.

It is important to confidently move ahead into our first calling or career. We do not have to be stymied by the misconception that it will be the only career or calling we have till retirement.

---

10   Philippians 4: 13

As we see from the life of Joseph, many careers or occupations brought him to the zenith of his last career (that of the Prime Minister of Egypt). The same is true for most people. God is developing and maturing us not only for the careers or professions we will obtain but also for His kingdom purpose that we will ultimately fulfill His destiny in the best possible fashion.

Following in the Family Tradition

Of course, not all of us struggle with indecision. Many people follow the example of a successful parent into a generational profession. I have noticed that many careers are continued on in families. For example: Engineers' sons and daughters often follow their parents in the engineering field, academics often produce the love for higher education and academic pursuits in their children, doctors beget doctors, and so on. At times family pressure to carry on the generational tradition can be such that people slot into careers that they are not suited to, or have no enjoyment in, so they lack the passion it takes to devote energy that would see them reach their potential in that field.

I have also noticed the opposite take place when a child will deliberately choose a vastly different career than their parent. This is not always because of their true passion or aptitude but sometimes as a reaction to something negative concerning the parent or career they have witnessed. So we can see there are times we need to examine and deal with our attitudes about family callings and generational careers in order to be free to discern our course of action. Often these responses to generational attitudes about calling are under the surface, but God wants to correct anything that keeps us from becoming all we are designed to be.

Check the Baggage

If you are feeling stuck in indecision about your calling you may like to take a few minutes to complete this journaling exercise[11].

"Lord why am I stuck? Please speak to me about my fears or concerns."

_____

_____

_____

---

11   If you are not familiar with listening to God through two-way journaling please see Appendix 2

Hindrances & Negative Expectations

Our insecurities can be very big hindrances to stepping into the calling we are created for. Low self-worth can be an issue from childhood that follows us, preventing us from going on into the calling we are designed to fulfill. From low self-esteem come negative expectations about our future. Things such as thinking that we cannot learn, that we cannot accomplish any more than our parents did, that we will never succeed, or that we are not employable (due to our appearance, social status, or intelligence).

There are endless possibilities for negative thinking about ourselves. Many of these mindsets are deeply rooted, even hidden from our conscious minds. Some of our negative expectations have been planted by the words of others. Such words as: "You will never amount to anything", "You are stupid", "You are clumsy", or "You are just like ..." (a person who has some negative quality), will have a negative effect on our expectations of the future. Negative words spoken over us can effectively curse our future when we believe and act in reaction to them.

These hindrances, negative words, and negative expectations can be removed through prayer. As we ask the Holy Spirit to identify the lies or curses He will reveal them specifically so that we may renounce our belief in them, we then ask God to forgive and cleanse us.

1. Ask God how we have modified our behaviour or thinking to accommodate these lies (have we vowed inwardly to never do a thing, let something happen, act like someone who hurt us, vow not to try or to give up).
2. Repent of all vows (Scripture tells us to make no vows).
3. Receive the truth from God by asking Him what he says in response to the curse or lie we have believed.
4. Choose to live out of the truth by His enablement.

There are many methods of dealing with hindrances, which

cause procrastination around stepping into our calling. One such resource is the Restoration Manual, which is available through this ministry.

Destiny Exercise

The following is a suggested question to help uncover hindrances. You may use this prayer and exercise to begin the process.

Lord Jesus, what lies do I believe that hold me back from stepping into my God given calling?

_____

_____

It is best to pray the prayer below for each lie, negative expectation, or curse that Holy Spirit has revealed.

> *Lord I renounce the lie of _____ . Please forgive and cleanse me. I repent for believing and acting on this lie. Please cleanse me from any judgments or vows I have made regarding my calling. I forgive [Name those who either spoke or reinforced the lie, judgments, or vows]. I choose to forgive myself for making choices, having negative expectations, or cursing myself because of lies.*

After praying you could do the visual exercise below; this is designed to allow the truth of the prayers to realign your soul.

Picture yourself with Jesus and hand over to him the negative words, judgments, and negative expectations. Then ask Him to give you His perspective on these things. It may come in the form of picture or words of truth. Write down the truth and record how he corrected the negative expectations of your future.

Chapter 4: Personal Identity

Who am I? Ever asked yourself that question? We are more than our physical appearance, more than the opinions of other people, more than our personality, even more than our talents and accomplishments. We, being born into God's family, are sons of God. I could say daughters of God also but all of us, male and female, are "sons of God". Sons in the scripture were given the family inheritance to distribute and manage. The daughters were loved in Hebrew families but had a very different position in the dynasty. Sons at maturity could act as family representatives with authority over land, finances, and family holdings.

The sons of God have the privilege of being joint heirs with Christ and are encouraged to live from the position of reigning with Him in the kingdom of heaven on earth. Jesus showed us how that looks as He took authority over sickness, disease, the elements of nature, and evil spiritual powers. In the same way He managed the power of God through His earthly vessel (His human body), so we are told to live. This, dear brothers and sisters, is who you and I really are. We are hidden in God through Christ and will, as we agree with God's work, rise up into the realization of our sonship[12].

Knowing the truth is the beginning of being set free. We need freedom from the lies that keep us locked in the limitation of our humanity and block us from our God given identity. We begin to live in agreement with the truth as we not only hear truth, but also believe it. The truth will set us free but we must believe, then we can put legs to it because the Spirit of the Lord will empower us to act on truth. As we repent of believing that

---

12   Colossians 3: 1-4

we are only human and receive the truth that we are partakers of the divine nature[13] we align with the truth that will allow us to live as Sons of God. We are called to rule and reign as co-heirs with Christ. This high calling becomes a reality only as we integrate truth about our divine nature into our lives. Through the Holy Spirit's work within us we are empowered to live the reality of allowing Christ to rule and reign in our own souls and then gain authority in our sphere of influence.

The hindrances we may have in our soul are due to lies, unbelief, or false conceptions about who we are. These blockages to our true identity can come from past generations, lies or curses spoken over us, negative judgments, and expectations about ourselves and also tragic or painful events. All of these issues, as well as demonic interference, are corrected by God through the blood of Jesus Christ[14]. We can apply the cleansing as has been shown in the last chapter[15]. The process of agreeing with the truth of God and being freed from all lies and every demonic influence has made a tremendous difference in the lives of thousands of believers, well worth the time in prayer to receive restoration of our God given identity.

It is a wonderful exercise to ponder the family you have come from and to focus on the positive things you have inherited. When we put that together with the beauty of God's inheritance, as His children, our true identity begins to formulate. Following are some suggestions that will be helpful in directing your thoughts as you spend time listening to God's perspective on your identity and family inheritance.

---

13 We have the Holy Spirit living within our spirit.
14 Jesus sacrificial death and the shedding of His blood was the payment for all of our sins and short comings
15 *Restoration Manual* by Rev. Yvonne Prentice, is available to assist in working through spiritual blockages to growth in Christianity

Where Have I Come From

List the positive traits, blessings, and characteristics I have inherited from my mother's family line:

_____

_____

_____

List the positive traits, blessings, and characteristics I have inherited from my father's family line:

_____

_____

_____

God what positive traits, blessings, and characteristics have I inherited from You my Supernatural Father God?

_____

_____

_____

Personality

Every Mother could probably say that she could see the personality of her child from before the age of two. In fact, as I look back on our five children I can connect the personality of each child even to how they moved in the womb! We had five very different personalities among our children, who are now all over the age of twenty-five. Looking back, I remember that the more active babies in utero were those who became out-going, active, and extroverted people. Conversely those who were less active and more peaceful in the womb are quiet, calm, and more introverted, people now.

Personality is given by God but also forms or moulds around our experiences in life, as well as the environment in which we grow. We are more apt to grow strong and stable if we are given a good foundation of stability and consistency as children. We become wounded and emotionally stunted if our environment is unstable, emotionally polluted, or abusive. Often our expectations for the future are formed by what we see modeled by those around us, how we are spoken to as well as how we are treated. Self-image, whether it has been nurtured or stunted, can be moulded by the attitudes of others toward us, especially by those of our family members.

Once again God sent His son Jesus Christ to bring redemption through His blood, so that negative experiences from our formative years or environment can be healed and redeemed. God can turn around the things that the enemy meant for evil, those difficulties can be changed into something good and useful in the course of our destiny. We find an amazing paradox; those who endured great abuse can become the vehicle for wonderful ministries to those who are in the circumstances or environment that so harmed them.

God can and will redeem our personalities and reveal our hidden God-given identity. The person we were created to be is within us, in all his or her beauty and strength, waiting to step into the purpose and calling for which we were created. The process of unveiling our true identity is overseen by the

Holy Spirit. Holy Spirit has unified himself with our spirit. He cleansed us when we repented of past sins and invited Him to join with us, making our spirit His home. We are partakers of His divine nature, one with God, even though our soul may still have many issues; our spirit is in good order because of Holy Spirit's divine work. God is the only one who truly knows who we are, our full potential, and what we are capable of accomplishing through our union with Him. Therefore, it is by asking Him that we find our true identity. It is by living in union with the Spirit of God that our personality is formed into the image of Christ, as per God's original design.

Enter into His Rest

There is in our human nature a strong desire to preserve ourselves or our self-image. We all have ideas, hopes, and dreams to which we strongly attach. These human desires often drive us to work against the good and perfect purpose God has in mind for our lives. It is our work to turn toward God and submit to Holy Spirit's leadership. This turning and submission is actually the discipline of entering into His rest. Resting in the sufficiency of God's power and leadership in every aspect of life is not easy or automatic for most of us, but it is the way Jesus exemplified. Jesus lived a yielded life, doing only the will of His Father in heaven. It is our part as His modern-day disciples to follow His way. This life style, of turning to God and only doing what the Spirit of Christ speaks to us, is the life of harmony, union, and peace with God. Through the life of union with God we are ushered into our true identity. Our purpose and calling will manifest along the way. Our destiny will be fulfilled with honour due to this life of rest in, and agreement with, the power of God to accomplish His good plans.

Entering the rest that God would have us live in is achieved as we lay down ambitions and ideas of self-actualization in favour of God's plans. We need to cease from human effort or striving and instead learn to flow in agreement with God. This is what God has wanted for each one of His people that we will enter into His rest[16]. As we live from His rest, resting in His power and ability to accomplish through us His destiny, purpose, and calling, we begin to live a supernatural lifestyle. Rest allows God to activate His power through us so that we realize the scripture stating, "I can do all things through Christ who strengthens me"[17].

---

16   Hebrews 4: 1-11
17   Philippians 4: 13

Who Am I

Do this quick personal assessment yourself and then have a loved one or safe person do it for you also. Finally, on the last copy ask God which characteristics He sees in you. Check the traits you have noticed in yourself.

Personality Survey: Self-Evaluation

- ☐ introvert
- ☐ extrovert
- ☐ spontaneous
- ☐ methodical
- ☐ meditative
- ☐ expressive
- ☐ leader
- ☐ team player
- ☐ independent
- ☐ good listener
- ☐ wise advisor
- ☐ generous
- ☐ moderate
- ☐ compassionate

- ☐ helpful
- ☐ supportive
- ☐ truthful
- ☐ assertive
- ☐ advocate
- ☐ creative
- ☐ musical
- ☐ mechanical
- ☐ analytical
- ☐ concise
- ☐ poetic
- ☐ merciful
- ☐ mindful
- ☐ gentle

- ☐ positive
- ☐ hardworking
- ☐ peaceful
- ☐ tactful
- ☐ direct
- ☐ kind
- ☐ forgiving
- ☐ honest
- ☐ integral
- ☐ motivated
- ☐ articulate
- ☐ thoughtful

Personality Survey: How Others See Me

Please indicated each of the positive traits you have noticed in:

_____

- ☐ introvert
- ☐ extrovert
- ☐ spontaneous
- ☐ methodical
- ☐ meditative
- ☐ expressive
- ☐ leader
- ☐ team player
- ☐ independent
- ☐ good listener
- ☐ wise advisor
- ☐ generous
- ☐ moderate
- ☐ compassionate

- ☐ helpful
- ☐ supportive
- ☐ truthful
- ☐ assertive
- ☐ advocate
- ☐ creative
- ☐ musical
- ☐ mechanical
- ☐ analytical
- ☐ concise
- ☐ poetic
- ☐ merciful
- ☐ mindful
- ☐ gentle

- ☐ positive
- ☐ hardworking
- ☐ peaceful
- ☐ tactful
- ☐ direct
- ☐ kind
- ☐ forgiving
- ☐ honest
- ☐ integral
- ☐ motivated
- ☐ articulate
- ☐ thoughtful

Personality Survey: How God Sees Me

Practice Listening Prayer: Ask God, "What positive traits do You see in me?" Picturing yourself with Jesus often helps to hear His voice. Circle what you sense He is saying about you.

- ☐ introvert
- ☐ extrovert
- ☐ spontaneous
- ☐ methodical
- ☐ meditative
- ☐ expressive
- ☐ leader
- ☐ team player
- ☐ independent
- ☐ good listener
- ☐ wise advisor
- ☐ generous
- ☐ moderate
- ☐ compassionate

- ☐ helpful
- ☐ supportive
- ☐ truthful
- ☐ assertive
- ☐ advocate
- ☐ creative
- ☐ musical
- ☐ mechanical
- ☐ analytical
- ☐ concise
- ☐ poetic
- ☐ merciful
- ☐ mindful
- ☐ gentle

- ☐ positive
- ☐ hardworking
- ☐ peaceful
- ☐ tactful
- ☐ direct
- ☐ kind
- ☐ forgiving
- ☐ honest
- ☐ integral
- ☐ motivated
- ☐ articulate
- ☐ thoughtful

Living in union with God is the lifestyle that can benefit us in in the personal peace and fulfillment it yields as well as what we are able to achieve. Whatever is gained through human effort will have to be maintained through human effort; often ever-increasing amounts of energy are needed to keep the pace of what self-effort has produced. It is never too late to come back to God and refocus your life and desires. You may wish to re-dedicate your passions and desires by using the following prayer:

Lord Jesus I repent for any passion which is not of you [Name them]. Lord I submit my motivations to you, please mould my motivations toward your heart. Jesus, I give you the good passions and desires I was created to fulfill. I repent of trying to fulfill them in my own way, with my own understanding and effort. I dedicate my passion for [Name each love or passion], and ask that you develop in me Your understanding. Please give me your power to work along with your Spirit in these pursuits so that I will only do as you quicken me and so that I will live from agreement with your desires for me. In Jesus name, amen.

Prayer commitment made on

Signed

Passions & Dreams

Our desires and dreams are often planted by our Heavenly Father and can be deeply rooted in His plans for our life. As we connect with God and learn to submit our dreams for the future and passions to Him, we find our desires taking beautiful shape. If we allow the Master Designer to work in our souls, bringing us into alignment with divine purpose, we notice God will open opportunities for us to grow. He will expand our understanding and give opportunities for us to learn in the area we have passion for. God will also help us to see where these abilities fit in His kingdom plan on the earth.

I believe purpose, calling, and ultimately destiny, emerge as a by-product of our yieldedness. God moulds our desires, passions, and dreams working with them – not in spite of them. It is the moulding of human nature by the Holy Spirit in us that births God's Kingdom plans in us. The fears of some believers that God will ask them to do or go to places that are very opposite to their desires are often unfounded. I have noticed most of us are already in agreement with the way God wants to direct us because He originally seeded our desires within us. It is Holy Spirit who conforms us to the ways of God. He endows us with a deep desire to move in the direction of our destiny through the callings we are drawn to.

When human desire aligns with God's kingdom plan, we have a winning combination. However, if we allow human ambitions, self-effort, and striving to motivate and drive us we will be working against God's Spirit[18]. Selfish ambition and the need to "be somebody" side tracks and diverts our lives. Our ungodly thinking about good desires or pursuits, take us further away from agreement with God. Self-actualization will pervert our motives, even for seeking God. A simple example of this is when we only go to God for what He can do for us rather than to enjoy who He is. The pursuit of self-fulfilment is the foundation of striving to attain that which only God can give.

---

18   Zechariah 4: 7 (NIV) "Not by might nor by power but by My Spirit says the LORD Almighty".

We will never achieve the full potential of our lives if we focus on self, striving and working hard. What we achieve by striving and human effort will have to be maintained by much of the same. On the other hand that which God achieves by his power through us will have His momentum and kingdom power propelling it on to fruition[19].

---

19   1 Corinthians 2: 9 (NLT) "No eye has seen, no ear has heard, and no mind has imagined what God has prepared for those who love him".

Why Am I Here

Discerning My God Given Passions and Dreams: Answer the following questions

What abilities have others seen in me?

_____

_____

Has God given me a dream?

_____

_____

What aspect of God's kingdom do I long to see come to earth?

_____

_____

What do I see around me that makes me righteously angry or indignant?

_____

_____

What personal hopes and aspirations are yet to be accomplished?

_____

_____

What have I dreamed of doing since childhood?

_____

_____

I am happiest when...

_____

_____

I lose track of time when...

_____

_____

If money and time were not an issue what would I love to do?

_____

_____

What, if any, are the walls or hindrances that prevent me from doing what my heart desires?

_____

_____

Chapter 5: Gifts from God

Every human being ever born has been fashioned in the image of God[20]. We are designed with destiny and purpose in mind and so, built into our very being are spiritual and natural gifts and talents. We begin our examination of these gifts and talents with the spiritual gifts God gives in order that our lives may produce His kingdom purpose on earth.

Scripture provides three different lists of the gifts or special abilities that come with the Holy Spirit. The compilation of the lists from these scriptures is as follows: service, teaching, prophecy, encouraging, giving generously to meet the needs of others, administration (leading or governing), mercy, word or message of wisdom, word or message of knowledge, faith, healing, working of miracles, discerning of spirits, tongues (language unknown to the speaker), apostles, evangelist, and pastor. This power (Greek *dunamis*) is resident in Holy Spirit and continues among us today. As we invite Him to fill us and yield to His greatness we will also be endowed with this same *dunamis* power.

Three Types of Gifts

The gifts are given in three separate lists. Scripture gives clarity as to the reason the lists are differently arranged. 1 Corinthians 12: 4-6 breaks down the differences:

- There are different kinds of gifts, but the same Spirit. (KJV: gifts)

- There are different kinds of service, but the same Lord.

---

20   Genesis 1: 27

(KJV: administrations)

- There are different kinds of working but the same God works all of them in all men. (KJV: operations)

Different Kinds of Gifts

Described in 1 Corinthians 12: 8-11 (Greek word for gifts here is charisma), this list refers to the supernatural manifestations produced by Holy Spirit including: healing, miracles, languages, and prophecy. These gifts are used to minister to others in the power of Holy Spirit. The second 1 Corinthians passage describes the correct use of these supernatural gifts.

Different kinds of service: Described in Ephesians 4: 7-13 (Greek word for service or operations is *diakonia*). This list refers to the leadership roles which enable the body of Christ to learn, to grow and be nurtured into maturity. This list, known as the fivefold ministry gifts, includes: Apostle, Prophet, Pastor, Evangelist, and Teacher.

Different kinds of working: Described in Romans 12: 6-8 (Greek meaning of working or operations is *dore*, to move as time moves). This list refers to the gift God gives which moves or motivates us to act. This list is made of some of the gifts within the other lists and includes: prophecy, serving, teaching, encouraging, giving, leading, and mercy. We will begin our exploration of the gifts in detail by looking at the motivational gifts.

Motivational Gifts

God has given each of us a heart motivation that will align us with his purpose for our lives so that we will fit beautifully into his plans and mesh with the body of Christ. The motivational gift is given before we are born and is part of our spiritual DNA. We notice it before we come to know God and it is evident even in early childhood. When we give our lives to Jesus Christ and receive the Holy Spirit the motivational gift blossoms, heightens, and grows as we mature in God. Other supernatural gifts come as we yield and are filled by Holy Spirit. These are called manifestational gifts because they are an outward working of Holy Spirit as He manifests through us. The list of Motivational Gifts is as follows: prophetic, service, teaching, encouragement, giving, leading, and mercy.

Prophetic

Always passionate for truth a person motivated by the prophetic will not compromise the word of God. Prophetic people are ready to move when God is moving. They are often ahead of people, calling them to follow what the Lord is about to do. Prophetic people are often loners spending many hours with God, even preferring a solitary life. The Prophet delights in bringing people into Holiness and alignment with God's truth. The downside to this gift is that those with a prophetic motivation can be harsh or blunt with words and can be tempted to bitterness and offence if people do not receive truth or correction.

Service

These helpful people love to care for and meet physical needs to enable others to fulfill their mandate. They enjoy doing practical things. Their motivation is to pitch in and make things happen. One motivated by service is a team player who loves people and enjoys the fellowship of working for a common purpose. Godly servers live with integrity and their deepest desire it to enable others to flourish. They are generally selfless, hard-working, and quick to volunteer. The downside of this gift is that they can be easily ignored and or victimized by those who will overload with demands, or who will fail to acknowledge the personal sacrifices that are involved in serving others. They need to follow the unction of Holy Spirit and to do as Jesus did in their serving (He did only the will of His Father) and to allow themselves to set healthy boundaries.

Teaching

People with the motivational gift of teaching love to study, research, and impart truth. They lay a foundation of biblical principles for practical application. Teachers instruct from researched and proven sources and discern what needs to be corrected in order to alleviate problems. Teachers tend not to be as social and relational as people with other motivational gifting's, unless they see a purpose for it. They may be people who are content in solitude and study. The teacher prepares the body of Christ by giving a solid foundation to truth that others can build on. Teachers can become stuck in dogma and hair splitting over small issues (pharisaical spirit). They may lack in relational building skills and also find research fills hours of time to the detriment of time spent with God enjoying relationship with Him.

Encouragement

This gift brings people along in their journey of faith. People with the motivational gift of encouragement bring hope for the future to the body of Christ which enables people to go on into their calling. The Encourager brings exhortation through preaching and teaching from personal testimony and examples. Not afraid of preaching to the crowd, the encourager often becomes the life of the party who loves being in the centre of the action. They can find time management and personal retreat a challenge because of this tendency toward the company of people rather than alone time with God. Encouragers can be tempted to live in rejection, or the fear of it, and can be prone to people-please to gain acceptance.

Giving

This motivational gift involves networking and sharing resources, givers love to help others achieve their kingdom purpose. They often give of their own finances and also connect people with resources from other places. Givers are independent; they think long-term and look at the investment value in their giving. Givers need to learn to be discerning in giving; to be generous but not indiscriminate. The biggest challenge for the giver is to give from faith, not only from their own resources, but from the heart of God. Intimacy with God can be an issue for the giver, so God uses the need for wisdom in giving to draw them in to spending time with him.

Leading

This gift brings teams of people together for a common purpose. People with the gift of leading see the big picture and desire to release heaven`s plans upon the earth. They have many kingdom ideas and much vision. A leader is not usually one to volunteer, but will rise up into potential if called upon. They need the focus of God to narrow their sights and fulfill their part of a project. A leader is good at organizing all the pieces of a project but not always good at seeing it through to completion. The weakness of the leader is they can go ahead of God and others and act too quickly. Leaders need to learn dependence upon God by honouring God through their obedience to seek Him for timing.

Mercy

A person embodying the motivational gift of mercy is a lover of the body of Christ who nurtures, reassures, and brings healing to broken hearted people. A mercy gift fits well with every gift because mercy brings the heart of God into the equation, the gift of mercy is one that is "tuned in" to God's heart. This may mean that the person with the gift of mercy may 'feel' intuitively what God's heart for a circumstance is, but may have difficulty expressing how or why they know this. Mercy can see both sides of an issue, which allows them to bring grace, rather than judgement, when people are vulnerable. Yet, this may also cause the mercy giver to hold back correction when it is needed, which means that the mercy gift is best teamed up with another gift for correction. These people team wonderfully with the teacher, prophet or leader who are not as apt to feel the compassion of God for His people. The weakness of the mercy giver is they tend not to have a clear stance on values, but to seek acceptance from people. They can be tempted to keep peace instead of mercifully speaking truth.

Discerning Which of These Gifts Motivates Your Heart to Act

Following is a scenario that exemplifies how these different motivational gifts act in life. This example is helpful in giving us clues as to what our motivation is by describing how each of the gifts may respond to a friend who has fallen ill.

Prophetic

"What is God trying to tell you through this illness? Is there sin you haven't dealt with?"

This is the response of a prophet motivation as they seek to discover the spiritual implications of not being blessed.

Service

"Here's a little gift! I brought your mail in, fed your dog, watered your plants, and washed your dishes."

This is the response of a server motivation as they seek to demonstrate practical concern or assistance for others.

Teaching

"I did some research on your illness and I believe I can explain what's happening."

This is the response of a teacher motivation as they seek to research the roots and solutions.

Encouragement

"How can we use what you're learning here to help others in the future?"

This is the response of an Encourager motivation as they seek to use experience as a stepping stone for further growth.

Giving

"Do you have finances to cover this illness and resources to cope with your needs? If not I know of x, y, or z person or organization that will be able to help"

This is the response of a giver motivation as they seek to network resources of God's provision.

Leading

"Don't worry about a thing. I've delegated your job to four others at work."

This is the response of a leader motivation as they seek to facilitate / accomplish the re-establishment of health.

Mercy

"I can't begin to tell you how I felt when I learned you were so sick. How do you feel now?"

This is the response of a mercy motivation as they seek to express sympathy and genuine love.

Ask yourself: "How would I most lightly respond in this scenario?"

Manifestational Gifts

The first listing of gifts noted in the 1 Corinthians 12: 4-6 passage is referring to the charisma or supernatural manifestations of the Spirit. These gifts or abilities empower us to minister in the revelations and miracles God wants. All of the gifts noted in these three lists can be manifested through us when needed. Most believers move in one or two regularly and become confident in their operation through them. For example, one may be born with the gift of mercy but often is able to move in prophetic words of knowledge and healing. The specific list of Manifestational Gifts is as follows: Word or Message of Wisdom, Word or Message of Knowledge, Faith, Healing, Working of Miracles, Prophecy, Discerning of Spirits, Tongues and Interpretation. These gifts only operate through the power of God and cannot be worked through human resources. Other gifts can be used through our natural resources and supernatural unction such as; teaching, serving, giving, encouraging, administration, mercy, apostle, pastor, and evangelist. It is however important to note that though we may be able to perform these functions in our natural abilities we will not be moving in agreement with God's preference, which is that we operate in and through Holy Spirit's unction and power. This is accomplished by continually yielding to Him, inviting Him to speak, and receiving His direction in our operation of our abilities and functions.

Word of Knowledge, Wisdom, and Prophecy

These gifts of the Holy Spirit are known as "revelatory gifts", meaning they supernaturally reveal things not naturally known without God's disclosure.

Spending time in God's presence will transition us into His supernatural gifts and abilities. As we agree with God deeply, listen for His voice, commune with Him daily and act on His promptings, the revelatory gifts of Holy Spirit will become stronger within us.

My experience with these abilities began after I was initially filled with the Spirit of God and as I devoted myself to Jesus, communing with Him each day. I began to receive words of knowledge and with them, words of understanding flowed from my spirit. These revelations first began while praying for others, and later came more spontaneously, without any effort on my part (I did not ask for this knowledge and I was not in prayer or soaking). These revelatory events came both spontaneously and as I prayed for others.

I have discovered some helpful tips through operating in these gifts that I will share now, in the hopes they will smooth your transition into the flow of these gifts of Holy Spirit.

Word of Knowledge

My own experience with word of knowledge is that information I do not naturally know about a person is just there. This information comes into my thoughts usually before I even have a chance to look for Jesus or to hear God's voice with regards to a person. Word of Knowledge can come in any of the ways God speaks (not only in words as the name implies); it is basically information that is given to me by God. This knowledge comes to mind as soon as I begin to think of praying for the person or situation.

As I have mentioned, a word of knowledge feels like I already "know" specific information about someone, although there is no natural way I would have had access to the information. I then talk to the Lord about it, asking Him whether I should share it as it is (raw, so to speak). According to His prompting, I may share it uninterpreted (e.g. "I see a black dog bearing its teeth. Have you encountered such an animal in your life?"). The recipient can then confirm whether this was indeed a word of knowledge (e.g. "My aunt has a black dog, and it tried to bite me last month"). At that point, I am free to go on with what the Lord is saying for them, having perhaps now established a better connection with the individual.

This approach allows the prophetic word which may follow a greater likelihood of being well received: the word of knowledge came first, showing that God really knows about the recipients' life, cares about them, and wants to communicate with them through us.

On the other hand, if the revelation does not appear to be a word of knowledge (e.g. "No, that doesn't ring a bell, I haven't had an encounter with a black dog"), then we have the opportunity, as God leads, to give interpretation to the metaphor, as in the following section.

Word of Wisdom

While basic wisdom is the application of knowledge and experience, supernatural wisdom involves interpretation and application given from God, not from human thinking. Sometimes without natural knowledge or experience, we just sense how to handle a situation thanks to direction and insights that are from God. Supernatural wisdom is delivered to us Spirit to spirit, not from our natural reasoning but from God's unlimited resources.

A word of wisdom very often arises similarly to a word of knowledge, in that we already seem to "know". With a word of wisdom, Holy Spirit also provides guidance regarding how to put into practice the revelation, so that, we feel strong direction as to what to do in a particular situation. Even if we don't have all the information that human decision-making would require. Word of wisdom supernaturally anoints us to act or to counsel someone.

At times I have experienced this download of supernatural wisdom and, without realizing what has happened, have spoken wise words from the flow of Holy Spirit. My mind has thought, "Wow this is very good, I need to write this down so I don't forget!" while God's words bubbled up.

When God is giving wisdom, it is almost always something we could not have devised in human thinking. I have often experienced God's wisdom flow as I teach, providing practical application (for example, meeting specific individual needs which I am made aware of after the session). This supernatural flow of wisdom unlocks people's circumstances and brings to our lives God's anointed strategy and action plans.

There are occasions when we receive wisdom with time to ask the Lord about it and to wait for His response before we release words as His counsel. At these moments, it seems the timing of delivering this wisdom is important; if it is for us to deliver to someone else we need to ask for the appropriate opportunity to speak it. When a word of wisdom is given for our own personal circumstances, we need to ask God for the right time to enact what he has shown us.

Let us again stress the difference between good advice and the revelatory gift that is a word of wisdom. Although good advice can be godly and helpful, it is not supernaturally downloaded or discerned; it comes by experience and knowledge, so it is natural. While this does not necessarily make it bad or wrong, it is just not the same as a word of wisdom from Holy Spirit.

Human wisdom can sometimes cloud issues and even cause the revelatory prophetic word to become lost in the fog of too much information. Caution must be used especially in group settings: too much information can cause confusion. Confusion can be a tactic of the enemy, not at all helpful for those listening for God's words to them. While the enemy attempts to muddy the waters of understanding, God's supernatural wisdom brings clarity, peace and an action plan.

Prophecy

When our heart is connected to the heart of Jesus it allows us to feel the love of God towards the one for whom we are prophesying.

In my experience a prophetic word often comes when I am praying for a person, as I focus on Jesus and listen to God with regards to the person or situation. Prophecy follows as I simply pass on to others what the Lord is saying to me.

The prophecy may come in the form of words, pictures, impressions or some other way God wants to use at the time. Our part is to be open and sensitive to the Spirit of God within us. The words that flow from a spirit filled with the love and grace of God will be more effective and healing. On the other hand, if we are struggling to love the recipient, we need to be quiet; any revelation we have for that person may be tainted by our personal opinion or by some judgment or offense we have regarding them.

Of course, if we are speaking in the name of God, we need to exercise care! The Spirit of Prophecy is the Spirit of Jesus[21] so we need to be very close to Him, manifesting His love, truth, and peace, if we are to impart His heart to others. Please note: As some people do not understand prophecy or are offended by it, I usually first seek God for direction and wisdom as to how I should proceed with what He has spoken or shown me. It is best to ask God whether or not we are to share at all, as well as what to share – perhaps just a portion of the bigger picture we have seen is to be communicated. Sometimes, we need to pray into the revelation without necessarily speaking it out loud at all.

A practical example of the use of the revelatory gifts: The Lord may prompt me to interpret the word of knowledge, rendering it prophetic (e.g. "I see a black dog bearing its teeth. Could this represent a friend turning on you, not deserving the trust you have had in him or her?)" Note the difference here the prophetic rendition interprets the message rather than asking if the person has the black dog in their history. Here too, the recipient can respond as to whether this applies to them or not, with the potential of a greater opportunity for me to move forward with speaking on behalf of Holy Spirit for the individual (i.e. "God wants you to know that He…)"

Then perhaps a word of wisdom will follow such as "God is impressing that this person is wounded and needs understanding. You need to set safe boundaries for yourself keeping the relationship open but some distance is needed to keep it healthy.

Healing

All healing comes from God. Healing can be physical, emotional, or spiritual and in each of those areas God is the healer. Supernatural healing is more overtly a work of God as the scripture says it is a normal activity of those who follow Jesus[22]. There are many examples of the disciples of Jesus

---

21   Revelation 19: 10
22   Mark 16: 17 & 18

working healing miracles. Usually miracles of healing are outstanding such as bones mending or realigning instantly, pain instantly leaving, cancers leaving the body, as well as long standing illnesses or diseases being cured rapidly etc.

Miracles

Jesus performed many miracles where He caused the forces of nature to work counter to natural order[23]. The early believers did likewise and many people in our day have had the privilege of doing the same by God's supernatural power.

Tongues and Interpretation (Languages)

This supernatural gift comes in the speaking of an unknown (to the speaker) language, often called the "gift of tongues" and also interpretation of tongues. The languages can be in earthly and heavenly languages[24]. This supernatural ability is given to edify our own spirit by aligning our inner-man with the Holy Spirit. It is also a sign to others that God is at work especially if the language is earthly and understood by them. I have spoken in Bengali, a language I do not naturally speak or understand. The woman who told me was new to the gifts of the Spirit and also beginning to learn Bengali to better help the people she had been winning to Christ. She interpreted the language that I was using during a time of worship as a phrase in Bengali meaning, "to the beautiful One, the beautiful One who is among us". I was very blessed to be told what I had been singing and she was reassured that the gift of tongues or "prayer language" is from the Lord. She had naturally interpreted what she had learned because she knew the language, but there is also the gift of interpretation, which the Lord has given to me. Interpretation of languages in its supernatural form can come through inner-knowing where one receives the overall understanding of what God is saying and can explain the overall meaning. It can also come as phrases of English (or the

---

23   The record of Jesus walking on water is found in John14: 25. In John15: 32-38, Jesus feeds four thousand
24   1 Corinthians 13: 1

language of the interpreter), as spontaneous thoughts of the interpretation, whilst the speaker is talking in the unknown language. Tongues can also be interpreted prophetically by the next prophetic utterance that follows. The person who speaks in the tongue may receive the interpretation, or any person present may be given the interpretation.

Discerning of Spirits

The supernatural ability of discernment given by Holy Spirit informs as to whether the motivation of the person is of God, is their own human ambition or desire, or is a demonic source. The Discerning of Spirits gift also detects which demonic spirit is at work, so as to alert others as to the deception and to enable the binding of that spirit and to bring freedom to the person who is operating by that influence. This gift can operate much like Word of Knowledge being imparted by a thought from God in the mind. It can also be given by way of physical sensation (often pain or coldness). Discerning can be given by vision where by the person sees a name or a demonic form or darkness over the person or attached to them. Usually the gift is given to those involved in healing and deliverance ministries but can be given to any who are ministering as needed.

Administrative Gifts

The list of service or administrative gifts is both tools for ministry as well as being the calling or vocation of individuals. Administrative gifts are as follows apostle, prophet, evangelist, pastor, and teacher. As the name implies the Administrative Gifts are leadership areas which lay a solid foundation for the community of Christian believers (Church). These abilities are for the benefit of God's people to build them up and mentor them into greater confidence in living in agreement with the flow of Holy Spirit. On the one hand these gifts are graces given to enable us to; make new inroads, prophesy, evangelize, pastor and teach others about God. On the other hand, the administrative gifts enable leaders to direct the community of believers and to impart skill in the use of these abilities.

The Apostle

The apostle is a gifting that breaks new ground, starts new things, and implements strategies for God's kingdom to increase in areas where darkness pervades. The anointing to take ground in new areas is an ability which can be used in the body of Christ, in business, in the arts, in government, in technology and more. This ability can be seen even in the secular world, for example successful businesses whose leaders begin ground-breaking work, or people who make huge gains in technological areas which change the lives of many. These apostolic gifts are God-given whether they are used for His kingdom or not. Those of God's people who are gifted to break new ground and orchestrate new kingdom strategies are often accompanied by signs wonders and miracles which authenticate their gifting and create an environment of faith. This enables other believers to be confident and join the team to accomplish the large tasks God has called the apostle to do. Apostles often start large movements of God which bring God's kingdom into new levels of recognition and accomplishment in which God is given honour and glory. The large scope and big picture of the apostle needs to be tempered by the humility of Christ and patience for those who may be slow to act on the direction of Holy Spirit.

The Prophet

As mentioned, prophecy is a gift of discerning the word of the Lord, which can come through any or all of the senses, (see Chapter 5) and making His word known. It is a gift that enables us to hear God for our own edification, encouragement, and comfort as well as to direct us personally. The anointing rests upon every believer, though we do not all move in prophecy regularly. The prophetic person brings encouragement, edification, and comfort to those to whom the Spirit directs whether they are Christian or not. The administrative prophet is one who is accurate in predictive and or revelatory prophecy and who is enabled by the Holy Spirit to supernaturally impart the prophetic gift and mentor others in prophecy. The prophet's heart is passionate for the truth of the word of the Lord to be followed. The prophet needs to drink of the love and mercy of Jesus and to move in grace for others who may be slow to act upon prophetic direction.

The Evangelist

The evangelist is a gift which draws those who do not know Jesus Christ into the knowledge of God and relationship with His Spirit. All Christians can operate in the ability to evangelize by the Holy Spirit's power however some of us are supernaturally enabled to evangelize with the result that many people are drawn to God. Evangelists are able to lead them to Him easily and are naturally at ease sharing the Gospel of Christ. A more notable degree of this anointing is that the evangelist carries the ability to impart the anointing of evangelism to others. These people then become magnets for hungry seekers who are easily led to Christ. Evangelists love non-Christians into the kingdom of heaven. Evangelists tend to be 'edgy', they are often more comfortable in the company of non-believers than in church because their gift is not within the body but to reach out into the world and rescue the lost. Because of this they may have difficulty fitting the culture of traditional church, feeling more comfortable in non-traditional settings. They may not understand the need to nurture and encourage believers because God has given them a huge passion to reach out.

The Pastor

The gift of the Spirit which cares for, loves, and nurtures the people of God. Pastors are the tenders of God's garden. They are characterized by strong relational gifting and gracious perseverance with the imperfections of the growing body of believers. Many of God's people carry the pastoring anointing and love to care for and nurture people. They love to visit the sick and encourage people with acts of kindness, which is God's heart for all his people. Pastoring is not limited to caring for God's household of faith. Many with evangelistic leanings love to pastor those who are not yet believers. It is thus through the love and care of the pastoring gift that many people believe in the love of God and see the people of God as their new family and place of belonging. The gift becomes the administration, or leadership ability, when the pastor is reproducing those who pastor. The administration to reproduce loving shepherds of God's flock is supernaturally imparted and creates a community of God around the pastor, much like the 'magnetic' effect that the evangelist carries for non-believers. The difficulty for Pastors is where the line is between pastoring from the supernatural anointing and pastoring from human love and compassion. Burnout occurs when the supernatural is supplanted by human effort in loving and caring for people. When Holy Spirit is leading and empowering much less natural activity or human effort is seen, however, God's kingdom is being produced and flourishing as a result.

The Teacher

The administrative gift of teacher carries all the attributes of the teacher mentioned in the manifestational gift (see above) as well as the ability to impart the gift and passion of teaching, receiving revelation, and researching to others. The teacher is like the other administrative gifts, a foundation builder of the body of Christ. Teachers keep believers on track and aligned with the scriptures and the nature and character of God. They often have the ability to discern errors that could erode the foundation of truth and bring clarity to root problems. They are able to explain truth and encourage the body to correct and move into a better understanding of how truth can be applied. The teacher in this capacity often has the ability to clarify the larger working of God's kingdom bringing the people of God into agreement with the plans and blue prints of heaven.

Discerning My Spiritual Gifts

Motivational Gift
Please speak to me about the gifts You have given me. What gift have you given me to motivate me to in life?

_____

_____

_____

Revelatory Gifts
Suggested questions for meditation: Holy Spirit what do you want to say to me about your revelatory gifts?

_____

_____

_____

Speak to me about my participation in the use of Your gifts of revelation:

_____

_____

_____

Administrative Gift
Ask God which Administrative gift He has given you. Ask Him where you fit in the area of fivefold administrative gifts.

_____

_____

_____

Chapter 6: Talents & Skills

Scripture tells us: "Every good and perfect gift comes down from the Father of heavenly lights[25]." We can be sure that the natural talents we have come from God just as much as the spiritual gifts do and, that as we dedicate these talents to Him, God will anoint them to be useful and productive in kingdom work.

There are so many natural talents too many to mention all. However, some examples are listed as follows: Mechanical trades, computer sciences, culinary arts, visual arts, performing arts, language arts, craftsmanship, scientific, mathematical, biological aptitude, sportsmanship, musical talents. Often God uses the marriage of our natural talents and spiritual gifts to produce life giving ministries.

Following is an example of how natural abilities and passions can become a spiritual blessing which fulfills kingdom purpose through dedication to the pursuit of God in every area of life.

My natural ability of sewing has been a blessing to many people spiritually through the prayer blankets God inspired me to make. I have always been creatively artistic, a God given talent which surfaced in my childhood. The early passion to create led me to enjoy the process of sewing which l began to learn from my mother who was a gifted seamstress. I began to create clothing for my dolls and as I progressed I made my own clothing. Eventually I took college training in fashion design, textiles, and clothing construction. As a young woman in my early twenties I started to work in Bridal sales which also involved some seamstress work. Later I taught sewing

---

25   James 1: 17

and fashion design for many years. I also had the privilege of teaching art history and technique to home educated children in our home school co-op group.

When I became a Christian one of the first areas God put his finger upon to bring right focus and alignment with His heart was my passion for fashion. He taught me what was pleasing to Him and how I needed to focus on modesty and inner beauty instead of outward appearance. He moulded my passion toward His desires for me. As I grew in my friendship with God His Spirit continued to draw me deeper into the desire to please Him and live in greater agreement with His purpose for my life.

When at last I was filled with His Spirit in spirit baptism (which came some 20 years into my Christian experience) God began a major renovation of my soul. He activated spiritual gifts such as prophecy, word of knowledge, word of wisdom, healing, and languages. He intensified the motivational gift of teaching which had always been my favourite occupation. After some years of seeking more intimacy with God through spiritual disciplines of fasting, stillness, meditation[26] and listening prayer God birthed in me the prayer blankets and soaking ministry I continue in today. The blankets utilize the creative and artistic talents I had developed in sewing, along with spiritual gifts of prophecy, word of knowledge and word of wisdom which came supernaturally at the infilling of my spirit by God's Holy Spirit.

The manifestational gift of teaching has continued to grow and operate, now more from the spiritual gift of teaching, rather than only from the natural ability. Holy Spirit now is able to teach through me (His vessel) as I yield to His promptings and voice within.

God has given every person talents to be used in the anointing and power of Holy Spirit. Each of us has skills abilities and talents which we may allow God to anoint for even greater

---

26   See Appendix 3 for description of Biblical meditation

purpose.

What Are My Abilities

List your Talents and Skills below:

_____

_____

_____

_____

This part of the action step will enable you to put together who you are now. The following chart is divided into four areas we have covered. Your list of talents and skills (above) can be transferred to the text box provided. Use the information in action step 1 (your eulogy) to help define the list for passions and dreams. Action step 5 (personality survey) will enable you to fill in your positive personality traits. Working through the spiritual gifts (Action Steps 7, 8, and 9) will enable you to identify your motivational, manifestational, and administrative spiritual gifts.

Once you have completed the Chart above take some time to listen to God about who He has created you to be. Record what you sense He says to you.

_____

_____

_____

_____

_____

If you would like to rededicate your talents to Jesus Christ and participate with Him to bring kingdom blessing to the lives around you pray the following dedication prayer:

> *Thank You Lord God for the natural abilities and creativity you have blessed me with for [Name the natural abilities you have noted]. Lord Jesus I repent of any ungodly use of these talents and creativity in the past. I ask that you cleanse me of all sin. I give you now every talent and gift in my life [see yourself giving these talents, gifts, and abilities back to Jesus]. Lord I dedicate myself in all I am, the gifts, talents, creativity and abilities you have given to me. I ask you to anoint and empower and renew so that I may operate in them by yielding myself to your Holy Spirit. In the name of Jesus Christ my Lord, amen.*

Ask God to speak to you about how He sees the gifts He has given you and how He wants you to grow in the use of them:

_____

_____

_____

_____

Chapter 7: Additions & Distractions

Detours, Side-Tracks, Bunny-Trails & U-Turns

Being focused on God does not mean our lives are all work, or that all of our work has to have an overtly spiritual edge to it. God is relational; He invented family. Community is His idea, so we can be assured that spending time enjoying people is part of being God-centred. Having noted that, it is often a need for people and for their approval that drives our relationships and focus. Our enjoyment of people could be motivated by self centered need rather than God's love. A needy soul will lose the ability to discern the best use of time and opportunity. Personal neediness will drive us to distractions, side-tracking our calling, even veering us off our divine purpose (to know God and make Him known). Being driven by our needs instead of being satisfied by God can cause us to follow unproductive bunny-trails.

When God Posts a Detour Sign

Detour of Simplicity

We have said living a God-centred life is not one totally void of fun and human company, however, many of us are called to the disciplines of solitude and simplicity. These disciplines are not always comfortable or preferred by our human nature, which would rather crowd and fill our time with many things to satisfy our desire for importance or acceptance. God will often take us on a detour to refocus our attention as well as reveal our motivations. The nature of revelatory gifts is such that they require time alone with God. This enables us to learn to hear the heart of God and to become His friend. As the Scripture states: God does nothing that He doesn't share first with His servants (friends) the prophets[27]. For a time God may take us away from the clutter of busyness and people. Solitude with God has taught me to draw upon Jesus so I can enjoy times with others, not from a perspective of need for them, but with a fullness that chooses to give, rather than take. This time of detour is a privilege, however many of us struggle with solitude due to the days (even weeks) which may be required. Yet I have discovered that God is at work in the simplified life; that solitude, pruning, redirecting, and changing my heart toward Him for companionship is what is needed to mature me. The discomfort of loneliness can draw us to the secret place with God and teach us God's sufficiency in meeting every need for companionship and significance.

Many wonderful lessons are taught along the God ordained detours of our life. One of the ways I found to differentiate between a God detour and a mistake, or bunny trail, is that detours are not optional. We have not much option to choose whether we are going on a detour. Just like when the road crew redirects traffic, because the road is impassable, so it is when God takes us aside to be worked on. We must go. He makes it almost, if not entirely, impossible to avoid. When we arrive at our destination, having followed His detour directions, we find we have grown in spirit, character, and faith. We find a new maturity within which is the needed component for our next kingdom assignment.

Examples of God's Simplicity Detour

Jacob when fleeing from his brother had a revelation of God at Bethel Genesis 28: 10-20. Moses when fleeing the Egyptians had a revelation of God in the desert of Sin. Elijah was fed by ravens at Sinai when fleeing Ahab 1 Kings 19. John the Baptist was alone in the desert before entering His calling. John the Apostle, on the Isle of Patmos, was given extensive revelations

---

27   Amos 3: 7

of the end times and of Jesus which he recorded in the book of Revelation. The Apostle Paul went into the desert for two years after his conversion before entering his calling. Jesus before being baptized was in the desert where he fasted for 40 days.

Examples for Humility Detour

The lives of Joseph and King David are among many in Scripture where God allowed people to go through humiliating circumstances. Both of these men needed God's discipline to bring greater maturity for their very public leadership calling. Joseph faced several humbling life circumstances[28]: being hated and almost murdered by his jealous brothers; being sold into slavery by his brothers; and serving jail time after being falsely accused of assault. David was also humiliated by his brothers[29], hated, almost murdered and hunted by King Saul[30]. David also felt the need to hide himself by faking madness to an enemy king[31]. These humiliating circumstances worked the character qualities that God desired in these men, as well as bringing focus and dependency upon God. The humility detour enabled both Joseph and David to be the kind of men the Scripture calls "heroes of the faith[32]."

God is more interested in the process of growth in our character than He is in our progress toward achievements.

Side-Tracks and Bunny-Trails

Distractions can take many forms. I have noticed through my own journey, as well as in the lives of many others, the tendency to wander. It is important to realize many time and energy wasting deviations are actually distractions sent by our enemy to take our focus from our Kingdom work. The enemy's

---

28   These experiences are recorded in Genesis 37-41
29   1 Samuel 17: 28-29
30   1 Samuel 19-22, 24 and 26
31   1 Samuel 21: 10-15
32   Hebrews 11

strategy, to confuse and discourage, can come in many forms. For example: Pride can dial our number (so to speak) so that our ambition takes us off the God-path and onto a bunny-trail of selfish pursuit. We may begin to focus on minor things, becoming bogged down in details, which side-tracks us from the important tasks.

In this chapter I have listed some things that can cause us to side-track, to veer off onto bunny trails, and to make it necessary to U-turn back onto God's course.

Sin Issues

For the Sons of God[33] sin no longer prevents us from living for God. Sin does create problems for us, and for those around us, because it has consequences. Sin can cloud our decision making and side track our focus. Sin keeps us from coming to God, but it does not keep God from us! As far as our relationship with God is concerned, all we need to do is repent (turn away from sin, and go back to God). It is the turning away that most people find difficult because many times there is an underlying cause. Inner-healing and deliverance will remove the root cause if we are determined to be done with our sin[34]. I have found when we hate sin, God will empower us to stand in His grace and give us the power to resist further temptation.

Self-Focus

If we fix our eyes on Jesus as the Scripture commands[35] we find our focus to be in line with God's plans for us. When we fix our eyes on self, we focus on the inabilities, short-falls, and inadequacies of our ability. When we focus of our inabilities we

---

33   Those who are born-again, by trusting in the substitutionary death of Jesus Christ to pay their sin debt, are the children of God, sons and heirs to His kingdom.
34   Our method "Restoration Workbook- Restoring the Soul through Inner-Healing" is available through this ministry
35   "We do this by keeping our eyes on Jesus, the champion who initiates and perfects our faith" Hebrews 12: 2 (NLT).

tend to miss opportunities, hindering the calling of God on our lives. Yet, scripture tells us that through the power of union with Christ we can do all things[36].

There are two extremes when it comes to self-focus: Fear of failure, being at one extreme, in which low self-worth causes us to underachieve; at the other extreme, pride and selfish ambition which cause us to push ahead of God and away from His plan or timing. On our own we cannot do that which requires God and human working together. The solution to self-focus is God-focus. This is achieved by God and not by ourselves, as we repent and ask Him to be our focus. When we let go of our own ability or inability to achieve, giving our time and attention to Jesus Christ, we are given the grace to complete God's great purpose.

Striving in Human Effort

When God gives us a vision for our lives He intends to fulfill it himself, as we partner with Him. This means that we yield to his working through us, rather than trying to achieve the vision through our own effort. We could never accomplish the God-sized work He has in mind for us by our human effort. It is best, I have discovered, to yield and relinquish striving by resting in the sufficiency of God. Any work we begin by our effort will have to be maintained by ever increasing effort on our part...or by those who join with us. In contrast, I have learned to wait and allow God to open doors and He brings opportunities to me. These opportunities are enjoyable and the effort involved does not cause excess stress or burn-out. In fact, opportunities to serve God will come if I do not push or self-promote, but wait in humility. It is important not to despise small beginnings, but rather to prayerfully walk in step with Jesus into what He brings our way[37]. It is through this

---

36   Philippians 4: 13 (NLT) says, "For I can do everything through Christ, who gives me strength".

37   "Do not despise these small beginnings, for the Lord rejoices to see the work begin, to see the plumb line in Zerubbabel's hand" Zechariah 4: 10 (NLT).

intimate and prayerful journey that God trains and prepares us for 'bigger' and more challenging tasks or opportunities.

Set-Backs of the Past

Contrary to what most people believe, I find experience is not always the best teacher. Many times, the set-backs or failures of the past can, instead of educating us, become fear-producing hindrances. It is not by our human reasoning that we stay away from such pit falls, but by supernatural guidance and intervention.

God will allow our mistakes, which side-track, and bunny trails, which waste resources and steal our attention, so that we may learn of Him. He does not force us to stay focused, that is our part. However the best part of making mistakes is that we can learn from them. What happened last time does not have to happen again. As we learn to stay in close communion with Him, Jesus Christ will redeem and the Spirit of God will teach so that instead of fear of failure clouding our future the wisdom of God will enable us to plot a better course. Father God creates our destiny, because He is a loving God we can trust Him for wisdom and future plans.

Subversion of Corporate Destiny

God has given His people gifts in keeping with His plans for individual destiny and calling, as we have seen in chapter 5. He has also equipped the body with gifts for fulfilling a corporate purpose, calling, and destiny. Corporately, there are those gifted to lead and those gifted to serve, with many possibilities and combinations working together in the Body of Christ. It is a beautiful thing indeed when Jesus Christ is honoured and submitted to, as head of a ministry, business, or organization. Every person has a place, with each one working together in unity to bring the kingdom of God into the venture. Unfortunately, there are times when ambitious leadership begins to dominate and control God's people, subverting and diverting the team. This can redirect the team from serving

God and building His kingdom, toward building a man-made, man-serving organization. I believe God can, and often does, correct and redeem in such situations, but there are other times when He leaves, and the anointing of God is no longer over the project or organization. In fact there is a sad example in scripture you may want to explore as you ponder the issue of subversion of God's purposes by selfish goals. In 1 Samuel 4: 21, we read of the abuses of spiritual leadership positions by the sons of Eli, the high priest. In response to ongoing selfishness and abuse of spiritual leadership, and the nation of Israel's tolerance of these abuses, God's glory departed from the temple, symbolized by the capture of the Ark of the Covenant. In addition, God removed His anointing from Eli's family line, notably by the death of Eli's sons and by the simultaneous birth of his grandson, who was named Ichabod[38]. This story is a warning to leaders and team members alike that subverting God's plans can be disastrous for body or organization as well as for those in leadership. God has a plan and when we delight in His plan and purpose we will live in sweet fellowship with Him. Our lives will produce His kingdom on earth and our destiny will be fulfilled with honour.

Executing the U-Turn With Finesse

Often God gives warning by way of dreams, prophetic words, visions, signs, and circumstances before we go off on a tangent. He loves us and desires our obedience to His plan, but He does not force us to listen. So, even though we have been warned, we can choose to wander off into some seemingly enticing or exciting venture. Sooner or later we discover it is not where we are called to work. The problem is what to do, and how to get back on track. I have found the best course is to admit my mistake to God, my fellow workers and family and to ask forgiveness of all. The U-turn takes courage but when you consider the waste of time, energy, money, talent and many

---

38   Ichabod means "the Glory has departed from Israel" (1 Samuel 4: 21).

other losses, the sooner we humble ourselves and admit the error, the better everyone will be. Pride is a hard task master. Pride would love to push you on, but humility is where the blessing lives.

The best approach to getting back to where God wants you is to:

First Pray Through Any Hurts

Forgive those who may have wronged you causing you to be side-tracked from God's direction. Forgive yourself for being mistaken in your direction. Give up any judgments you may have made against others. Ask God what He wants you to learn through this journey and what He is teaching you about listening to His voice.

Return to the Last Place You Experienced the Presence of God

At times we can be so discouraged or annoyed with ourselves that we retreat into self-pity or self-abasement, neither of which is Godly. Jesus died that you may have abundant life, not so you would live in regret. Once we have repented and returned to God all we need to do is allow Him to position us again, so we can go on. Many times we have learned from our side-track and are actually more mature from the experience. Like Moses we must realize that without the presence of God on our journey, we cannot accomplish His plan and so we need to wait till He moves with us[39].

Wait and Be Still

We need not beat ourselves over and over, just return to our place with God, and wait for further instructions. Often it is from the place of waiting that we departed anyway. Our work is to wait patiently and learn from Him. Maturity takes time. Remember how a potter positions the clay in the centre of the potter's wheel and works the clay over and over till it is smooth

39   Exodus 33:12 -18

and mouldable. The potter is patient, knowing all good things come in time. It is the clay's job to stay put and allow the moulding process. The death of our own plans and ambitions takes trust, that the potter is good and loves us. Trust and faith in God enables us to yield to His ways. The work of allowing God to change us is a discipline more valuable than we know and essential to our growth.

When God Opens a Door – Walk Through

It may seem obvious that when the Lord opens the next opportunity we would move ahead, so why would this be my next point? Often there has been a cost to our little side-track or bunny trail. A lack of confidence in our ability to hear God, and damage done to our faith level, may be a residue over our enthusiasm to follow God. If we are unsure of the grace of God, we may feel our track record with God has damaged His trust in us and our friendship with Him. I assure you this is not so. The grace of God depends upon His love and faithfulness not ours. We will never be able to keep ourselves in grace, because grace is not grace if it is watered down with human works. "Grace has to be drunk straight" as Robert Farrar Capon once wrote[40]. If we think we have any part in making ourselves more acceptable to God, we have believed in a life of works (Old Testament). Remember, "The law was given through

---

40   Robert Farrar Capon: "The Reformation was a time when men went blind, staggering drunk because they had discovered, in the dusty basement of late medievalism, a whole cellar full of fifteen-hundred-year-old, two-hundred proof Grace—bottle after bottle of pure distillate of Scripture, one sip of which would convince anyone that God saves us single-handedly. The word of the Gospel—after all those centuries of trying to lift yourself into heaven by worrying about the perfection of your bootstraps—suddenly turned out to be a flat announcement that the saved were home before they started… Grace has to be drunk straight: no water, no ice, and certainly no ginger ale; neither goodness, nor badness, not the flowers that bloom in the spring of super spirituality could be allowed to enter into the case."

Moses; grace and truth came through Jesus Christ[41]". We are not under the restrictions of law. When we make mistakes, go off on a tangent, or misunderstand the way to go, God's grace brings us back in line without any barrier between us and His presence. His grace restores us into our place in Him, ready to resume and move on with Him. This revelation of grace shows that God, not our work, will keep us connected with Him. It is foundational understanding which will enable us to live as Sons of God who do not doubt their father's love and acceptance.

Additional Insight: The Role of Prophecy

The Spirit of Prophecy is the Spirit of Jesus

Every born-again believer has the Holy Spirit living within them and all of us have the capacity to hear God for ourselves. Prophecy is a gift of the Holy Spirit where by God shares His heart through prophetically gifted people for others. Not all have the gift of Prophecy. As we have seen in the chapter on gifts we are each given generously gifts for different purposes to work together in the Body of Christ so as to build one another up. God speaks encouragements for today and for the future through His prophetically gifted people. It is the future or destiny predictions which I would like to address here.

Faith and Fulfilment

When we receive a prophetic word or predictive prophecy we need to remember, if the person is hearing God accurately, the prediction will come to pass. Whether we have faith in the words or not, if they were words from God, He will fulfill them. I have had prophecies from people which I did not believe would happen, mostly because they were impossible or very improbable. However, years later, these predictions did come to pass. To explain what I mean I will share a couple of examples from my life. I was given a prophecy in the washroom at a church that I would write training manuals and

---

41   John 1: 17 (NIV)

books. I had no inclination to do that and really didn't enjoy writing, so I didn't even give it another thought. Fifteen years later I have written four such books. The woman I met in the church washroom was not a famous prophet, just a willing voice for God. Another time I was ministering to women from very difficult backgrounds teaching them to soak in God's healing presence, when one of the women predicted I would be making soaking CDs. I did not believe it could ever happen as I am not musical, but a decade later, I have recorded three such CDs which God is using to soak people in His healing love. This woman probably didn't know she was prophesying she was untrained, in fact probably didn't even attend church. God still used her words to plant a seed that eventually bore fruit. A seed that I didn't water at all. A seed I didn't even have faith to believe.

Hope for the Future

There are times when a prophetic word does give birth to faith and incubates in our prayers. These times are often when we see no hope in our situation or we are desperate for fresh vision for our lives. I have heard many people say they were asking for some kind of pointer or sign from God when a prophetic word came to them. They took hold of the hope it gave and directed their prayers agreeing with the prophecy. Once again if the prophecy is truly from God it will happen. The thing about our agreement is that it gives us vision and courage to overcome while we wait. If we first put our faith in God, who is the power to perform prophecy. As we wait in faith before the prophecy has come to pass, our souls can rise up in expectancy and overcome the things which are overwhelming us.

My husband Bob and I have many wonderful experiences of this kind of help from God. Following is an account of just on such time: We were in very dire circumstances financially having five children to support and no income, we had little prospect of work for Bob. The situation seemed insurmountable and we began to feel hopeless. We were in a state of gloom one evening. I have to say you could almost taste hopelessness when, out of the blue, the Holy Spirit stirred within me. I felt the surge of faith rising up at the reminder Holy Spirit brought of a prophetic word we had been given a year earlier. A visiting prophet had called Bob and I out in front of the church and prophesied that we would be like Joseph; though we would go through trials, we would rise up victorious and be in a place of authority with the ability to provide for not only our family but others also. We took hold of each other's hands and laid hold of the prophetic promise in prayer. We declared to God, as well as any spiritual force opposing us, that we believed God for this Joseph word. No matter what our circumstances looked like, we believed God's promise over and above all else. We committed our future into God's hands. We were encouraged as God refreshed us with His hope. We woke the next morning to the phone ringing with the offer of a job to begin as soon as Bob could come. God has faithfully continued to move Bob from one position to another, increasing the income with each move and positioning him at the top of his career.

> *Faith is the substance of things hoped for, the evidence of things not seen. (KJV) Hebrews 11:1*

It seems that there are times God will surprise us with unexpected fulfilments of words we have not even believed for. At other times He waits to see if we will believe Him against everything the natural circumstances seem to declare. God is the boss. What He says is always true. Our faith will not make it happen but faith that God is not going to fail at fulfilling what He has said, will give us grace to wait in victory till the promise manifests. Faith believes; it does not look around for proof in natural circumstances, it simply trusts in the substance of the word of God to produce from nothing what He has spoken. Just as He did in the beginning when God said "Let there be Light." His word will not return void. God's prophetic word produces, just as it always has.

Responding to Prophecy

Having said all of this we do need to test whether a person is speaking from the Spirit of God or not. We can know by how the prophecy affects our spirit. Does it bring faith, hope, peace, and cause us to be more loving and to love God more? Are we drawn to be unified with our brothers and sisters, to be forgiving, merciful, gracious, and generous? If these questions are answered positively and the prophecy aligns with Scripture, it probably is from the Lord. On the other hand, if the prophecy produces stress, fear, suspicions, or criticism of others and we do not have peace over what has been spoken the prophecy is probably not from God. For more on this see Appendix 3: Testing Revelation.

The final Acid test of prophecy is this: A genuine word from God will be fulfilled. It may take a life time to happen but if it does not by the time our lives end then, my friends, it was not from God.

Tracking With God

You may have identified an area of your life where you have wandered from the course God wants you to follow. Perhaps you have already made the U-turn back on track but have regrets or hurts to deal with. Take some time to listen to God for His perspective on your situation. You might like to soak to receive or journal and ask God some of these suggested questions.

Lord give me your perspective on my current course of action. Am I tracking with You in every area of life or side-tracking in some way?

_____

_____

_____

_____

Jesus please speak to me about the side-track or bunny trails I have taken. What are you teaching me through them?

_____

_____

_____

_____

10   Where Am I Going

At this moment each one of us is at a particular point in the scope of our destiny. It helps to recognize and orient ourselves with the phase of life we are in. Whether we are beginning to discover who we are or entering the zenith of our life's work, it is good to take stock and see the value of our particular place. Every point along our journey demands different levels of attentiveness, energy, and focus. At each juncture of life our mental orientation or view of our circumstances can either help to spur us onward or it can hinder us. Below are some options to indicate where in life you are.

- ☐ Discerning my Calling

- ☐ Gaining experience for my career

- ☐ Pursuing education in my chosen career

- ☐ Completing education or training

- ☐ Looking for work in my area of calling

- ☐ Transitioning from one calling to the next

- ☐ Involved in a long-term project

- ☐ Content in my current calling

- ☐ Discontent with my current occupation

- ☐ Feeling stuck in indecision about calling

- ☐ Re-entering the work-force

- ☐ At home raising a family

- ☐ Beginning retirement

- ☐ Experiencing the death of my vision

Chapter 8: Finding My Life in Him

Jesus said: "If you cling to your life, you will lose it; but if you give up your life for me, you will find it" (Matthew 10: 39, NLT).

Paul wrote: "My old self has been crucified with Christ. It is no longer I who live, but Christ lives in me. So I live in this earthly body by trusting in the Son of God who loved me and gave Himself for me" (Galatians 2: 20, NLT).

These thoughts from the New Testament are just as radical now as when they were written centuries ago. They are counter to human nature. These thoughts are counter to the culture of those times, and still remain opposite to ours. In fact, the logical mind cannot make sense of such concepts, yet if we do not live them we will not fully take hold of the life God has for us.

Scattered throughout the Scripture we find a number of "God lovers" who found their lives in Him[42]. People like Abraham, Moses, David, Elijah, Isaiah, Mary, Anna, Simeon, John, Peter, and Paul. They gave themselves over to Him; abandoning their own ambitions, plans, hopes and vocations to live in agreement with Him for their purposes and callings. Each ultimately fulfilled their destiny. They grew up into their Sonship and, although they were not perfect, they gained deep abiding friendship with God. Their stories are examples of God's grace activated in imperfect lives. Their faith became reality, not only deeply within them, but noticeably changing the world around

---

42   Matthew 16: 25, Mark 8: 35, Luke 9: 24

them. In fact, it was because of the inner reality, of hearing the voice of God and growing into their friendship with Him, that these men and women fulfilled the amazing lives we read of.

The extreme example of this kind of life is found in Jesus himself. Jesus not only spoke the words of life, He embodied these words. Jesus Christ is the living word, the way of life, the truth lived out, and the life-giver. John 1: 14 (NIV) tells us that, "the word became flesh" and lived among us. The Way, Truth and Life lived out what He taught for the world to see[43].

There are also many lives which are "types" modeling the concepts of intimate friendship with God. The lives of Queen Esther and of Ruth are filled with spiritual metaphors illuminating God's redemption and people's submission to and love for Him. As well, the book of "Song of Songs," also known as "Song of Solomon," is a wonderful love poem that reveals a spiritual mystery described in metaphors and symbols. If the reader will ponder and meditate upon them, the symbolism unfolds a spiritual journey which those who would be lovers of God must travel.

How Can I Find the Person I am Meant to Be?

Let's consider the words of Matthew 10: 39 in context of finding our lives in Him. I do not believe God is saying here that we must deny our God given identity. Why would God give us personality and soul capacities if we are to 'kill' or deny them? No, I am confident God likes who He designed us to be[44]. By the way, He would like us to like who He designed us to be and to embrace our identity. Self-hatred is not from God. We must learn to love and accept who we are. Certainly, we do not love sin or the sin-nature, which is prone to turn away from God, but we do need to recognize that God sees us already perfected

---

43   John 14: 6

44   Genesis 1: 31 tells us that after God had finished his work of creating, he surveyed his creation and he said that all of it, including humanity, was good

and is pleased with His workmanship. If we reject ourselves we agree with our enemy who is the accuser and destroyer of the beautiful design of God in us. To the extent we accept ourselves, with our flaws and weaknesses, we can move ahead in our life journey, relying on God's power to work His destiny in us.

It is the self-centred life that the verse is pointing to. If we cling to our humanly inspired and humanly empowered, selfish ambitions we will lose the authentic spirit filled life God wants for us. We must allow God to kill the selfishness of our own desires and ambitions so that His life can flow through us. As Paul tells us the old selfish life is crucified with Christ (Gal 2:20). For our carnal nature to be crucified and the new nature of God to flow through we need to yield to His plan and come into agreement with the life plan of God which is empowered by the Holy Spirit. This life is not empowered by self-abasement or denying who we are created to be, but rather embraces who we are as the Holy Spirit moulds and forms us into our true identities.

Loving who you are and giving God permission to mould you is the beginning of finding your life in Him. There is only one you in the entire universe. You carry the image of God (in which we are all made) in a completely unique way. Your gifts, talents, passions, and desires are all put together in a one-of-a-kind package which God has wrapped into you and gifted to the earth. Only you can fulfill what God wants to express on the planet and His imprint deposited in you needs to be expressed so that His nature may be seen on earth. Who you are is important, special, and needed, so let the light, the spark of the Divine nature you have inside, shine for all to see. Remember this light is God's nature shining through you. Selfish ambition and self-centred focus defuses the beauty of the light we carry, and that is why we must allow the old nature to pass away and embrace fully our new nature as children of God.

Embracing Identity & Being Authentic

To truly embrace your God given destiny and purpose and to live out your callings, you must be comfortable with who you are. Embracing your identity is paramount to agreeing with God for the things He has for your life. Very often God's plans are much more than we could even fathom. In order for us to carry this God-sized vision we must be at peace with who we are. If accepting and embracing who you are seems impossible, and the thought of being open to allowing others to know the real you is frightening, you may need some inner-healing. This healing of emotional wounds will remove the lies and negative thoughts that interfere with embracing your identity. Through inner-healing I have personally moved from fear, hiding my true self, to being comfortable and confident with the real me. God can remove our blockages and restore our identity, as well as heal our wounded emotions, if we are willing to face our past hurts and bring them to Him.

No Knock-Off People Allowed!

Embracing who we are releases us from the temptation to copy others and allows us to be authentic. We will never accomplish our unique part of God's plan on earth copying the personalities of those we admire. God made you because He wanted a YOU, not two of someone else. Authenticity is essential to your participation with the kingdom of God on earth.

Throughout this book you have been discovering your identity and connecting with your hopes, dreams, and desires. You have looked at your roots, and observed where you are currently in life journey. All of these glimpses of you make up the unique person you are. God has fashioned you to fill the particular place only you can occupy. If we model ourselves on the character and attributes of anyone less than Jesus Christ, our perfect model, we could become a kind of human knock-off, not the valuable, and genuine person God made us to be. How disappointing to God. How disappointing to all those who are in need of our part in the earth.

You are unique, one-of-a-kind, a treasure from Gods heart. He has carefully designed every aspect of your spirit, soul and body because He has wonderful intent and purpose for you. As the scripture states by God's mighty power at work within us, He will accomplish infinitely more than we could ever dare to ask or hope[45]. Your part is to accept who He has fashioned you to be and live in His limitless abundance. This is the adventure of finding yourself in Him, that you come into agreement with His assessment of you and allow Him to unfold His amazing destiny through your life. In fact, "No eye has seen, no ear has heard, and no mind has imagined what God has prepared for those who love Him[46].

---

45   Ephesians 3:20
46   1 Corinthians 2:9 & Isaiah 64:4

Where Am I At

Dream on paper and record your process including your prayers:

If I could choose a career or ministry without concern for resource limitations what would I choose?

_____

_____

_____

What limitations prevent me from moving ahead into this dream?

_____

_____

Emotional limitations:

_____

_____

Financial limitations:

_____

_____

Current responsibilities that limit:

_____

_____

Educational limitations:

_____

_____

_____

Needed Skills: Research the skills and educational
qualifications you need to fulfill your dream. Record your
findings below:

_____

_____

_____

Emotional limitations: Often the unknown element about
the next step in your journey can produce fear or hesitancy.
Information can help to overcome these emotional limits. It
is also best to ask God for His perspective on your perceived
limitations and fears.

You may like to record His answers to your concerns.

_____

_____

Financial Research: God can financially equip you as you move
ahead into the next step of your journey. Your part is to find
out what your needs during that season will be, so do the
research, pray and watch for God's resources to come your way.
He may provide in a number of ways even by way of increasing
our hours of paid work, a promotion, or a tax refund etc. Don't
put limits on Him, just be ready to take action as the financial
door opens.

_____

_____

_____

Responsibilities: Sometimes we take on responsibilities that are not ours to fulfill. At times we are manipulated by the agenda of others to fulfill requirements which are not necessary. In these cases, we need to assert healthy boundaries to protect our time, energy, and resources, so that we have freedom to grow into the expansion God has for us. On the other hand, when genuine responsibilities need our time we must look not to avoid them but for creative ways to fulfill and work with our situation. Sometimes leisure time (such as television watching, recreational hobbies or sports) will have to be sacrificed short term in order to grow educationally and experientially. It will be worth the short-term sacrifice to fulfill your life goal. Journal about each of your current responsibilities asking God about them.

List your responsibilities

_____

_____

_____

Ask for God's perspective as to priorities

_____

_____

_____

Are there any responsibilities that you need to let go of in order to make room in your life for the next phase?

_____

_____

_____

12   Getting to My Destination

The following exercise is designed to take you into the next step of the journey into your destiny, purpose and calling. Prayerfully fill in the footsteps asking God to show you the next step. It is often said that faith is spelled R.I.S.K so if we are going to act in faith we will feel the emotions that go along with risk. It is okay to feel fear at the prospect of taking a risk and putting yourself into situations you have not experienced before, however it is not okay to let fear hinder or freeze you. Taking a risk is at times uncomfortable, but it gives God an opportunity to prove to you that He is able to strengthen you and bless you with success. Without action and risk, faith is theoretical. Without action, faith is not alive[47]. True faith trusts in God's strength and empowerment. Be encouraged to keep moving ahead in each area of your life. Whether it is growing in your artistic gifts by investing time in practicing them or registering in college, university or seminary to get the qualifications needed to fulfill your desire for business or ministry, you will find God faithful. He will confirm, steer, and guide you as you move by faith, trusting in His Spirit to prompt you.

From your work in Action Step 5, list what you sense God desires for your growth in these footsteps. What is the next step you could take to develop your gifts and talents, as well as personal and relational skills?

Gifts and Talents: for example, if you have musical skill and desire to minister through music what is the next step toward improving your skill and perhaps offering to serve in music ministry (Music next step: devote 1 hr per day to practice, volunteer to play at youth group or on worship team.

---

47   James 2:20

Gifts and Talents

_____

_____

_____

_____

Personal & Relational: You have identified personality traits and perhaps seen areas of hindrance or weakness in your ability to interact with others. God desires to heal and restore you. Ask Him how you can encourage this process. If for example you hurt others by being abrupt, He may show you a root to be healed, or give you a strategy to help.

Personal and Relational

_____

_____

_____

_____

Ask God to speak to you about your hopes for the accomplishments of your life and the legacy you want to leave behind. Are these hopes and dreams what He has for you? List the items you have written in the Eulogy from action step 1, then pray through them, asking God for His vision for you and how your life fits into His Kingdom purpose.

Your desires matter to God. Often it was Him who planted them in you. Our vision of how they will manifest or become reality can be warped or tainted by a negative self-image. In the first footprint list your God given desires from the journal exercise at the end of Action Step 1

My Hopes and Dreams

_____

_____

_____

_____

Ask God to align your perspective with His bigger Kingdom vision of your future. In the God's Vision footstep; ask Him to open your thoughts about your destiny. Fill in your renewed Kingdom purpose and vision.

God's Vision

_____

_____

_____

_____

The next step in my calling: From action step 7, ask God "What are you saying to me at this stage of my life about my calling? What do you say about the walls, hindrances, and limitations in my path? How can I position myself to step into the next phase of my destiny?" Fill in the footsteps with your answers in point form.

In the first footprint list your desired next occupation, ministry, or calling and beside it put any wall, hindrance, or obstacle which presently holds you back. For example you desire to teach but are not sure you are suited and do not have the educational qualifications so these things become a wall to your stepping into your next calling.

Calling Walls

_____

_____

_____

In this footstep ask God "What is the door into my calling?" For example, to move ahead into teaching the next step may be to upgrade skills or perhaps volunteer as a teachers aid to see if you are suited. List the steps needed and open the door by taking them.

Calling Doors

_____

_____

_____

Stepping into the Depths of God

The most significant realization of every person is that they need connection with God. Our growth in every other area is enhanced and flavoured by our spiritual life. The thing about growing in friendship with God is that it is not one sided. You cannot make it happen. God will not make it happen. Friendship is the union of His desire for you and your desire to know Him. God already knows and is connected with you. His part is done. If you have chosen to come to faith in Jesus Christ (made possible by His atoning sacrifice on the cross) you have Holy Spirit who is the teacher, counsellor, healer, comforter, as well as all peace, wisdom, understanding, power and knowledge. He is all you will ever need. The more closely you commune or connect with Him, the more His attributes will imprint on your thinking and personality. The fruit of the Spirit (love, joy, peace, gentleness, patience, goodness, faith, meekness, and moderation) will become the fruit of your life. Our life is truly found in union with God.

The next footstep is the most pivotal, the step that will cross the threshold into your kingdom identity. Take time to ask God to lead you into the truth about changes He wants you to make, yield to His promptings and ask Him to give you fresh vision for the key areas of your life.

Ask God how He would like to realign your thinking. Yield your mind and give Him your attention or focus, time and resources. Listen to Him for each area and record the ways He would have you adjust.

Relationships can enhance your love for God or detract from it. Ask God which relationships are healthy and life giving. How can you encourage these people to join you in your love and fellowship with Jesus. Ask God which relationships are not helpful. How would He have you respond? Perhaps changes or a need for new boundaries are required to correct unhealthy areas.

The Deeper Step of Dedication: Making more room for God by

rethinking my life.

Focus

_____

_____

Time

_____

_____

Resources

_____

_____

Relationships

_____

_____

Appendix 1: Listening Prayer or Soaking in God's Presence

The terms listening prayer, stillness, waiting on the Lord, and soaking in God's presence are terms for very similar practices within the realm of intentional times of spiritual intimacy. Stillness is being quiet before God, as is waiting for the Lord to interact with us. Stillness enables us to actively listen for God's heart when we pray. Soaking in God's presence is a current term for an extended period of stillness (usually one or two hours). Being still before God was practiced by the ancients and has many references in Scripture: Psalm 2: 1-3, Psalm 27: 14, Psalm 37: 7, Psalm 131: 2, Proverbs 1: 33, Isaiah 40: 29, Hosea 2: 14, Matthew 11: 28-30, Luke 10: 39, Hebrews 4: 9-11.

Becoming still is the process of quieting the inner being. To accomplish inner quiet we often need to settle our outer distractions and then to focus inwardly. We move our attention inward, from the outer body to quieting the soul (mind, will, and emotions), so as to commune with the Holy Spirit who indwells our human spirit.

In order for us to enjoy communion with God, to hear His voice, we need to hush the noise around us and within us. Following are some simple steps that may assist you as you begin to learn to become still and hear God.

Allow Time

As you learn to relax and meet with God you will need to dedicate some time to the process. Time constraints can cause unrest. Clock-watching is a distraction which can be removed by setting a timer. Give yourself 10 to 15 minutes to settle.

Remove Outer Distractions

It is best at first to be alone, as electronic devices, phone calls, or the movement of other people and pets will cause interruptions. Gather things you may need: pen, notepad, a glass of water and perhaps a blanket for warmth.

Make yourself physically comfortable, so that bodily discomfort will not become a distraction. Bodily rest can be a position of lying down, sitting, standing, or walking. While each person has a preference for physical comfort while resting, choose a position that is different from your normal sleep posture. For those who feel most relaxed while walking, choose a quiet, solitary place to stroll.

Remove Inner Distractions

Relax, put a little smile on your lips. You may want to whisper the name of Jesus several times to focus your thoughts. Perhaps you will not need any further steps before you begin to sense God.

For some, however, this is when the mind begins to flit about or go into activity. Stillness of mind is not emptying the mind of thoughts but quietening the mind to focus on the presence of Jesus. Don't try to force the quieting of the mind, just listen to the thoughts and see what the issue is. If you need to address distractions of the mind, ask Holy Spirit, "What are my thoughts?" Listen to the thoughts that flow from the question. He will reveal any area of concern. Listed below are common concerns and how to quieten them:

For Worry

Give the concern over to God in prayer. Tell Him you trust Him to hold the issue (or person) for your time together. Picture the concern in God's hands and command worry to be silent in the name of Jesus.

For the To-To List:

Simply write the list down and allow your mind the peace of knowing you will not forget but will get to the list later.

People For Whom You May Pray

Even the needs of others must be put on hold for the time being. Just make a note of the names and purpose to pray for them. This is your time to personally connect and hear God's heart for you.

Sin-Consciousness

Awareness of sin and our own inadequacies can be a barrier to meeting with God. God has provided very excellent help for us in that Jesus has more than paid for our debt with His sinless life poured out on the cross. Just bring yourself to Him afresh and agree with Him for your cleansing and restoration. Receive your forgiveness. Allow Him to wash over you in loving acceptance and move into communion with Him unhindered.

Remember that condemnation, guilt, and shame are not sent from God. He takes you as you are. By His precious blood, you are now fully accepted into His family as a son and heir. Your inheritance is now to fully enjoy your Father, and allow Him to fully enjoy communion with you.

Dedication Prayer

You may want to use the following prayer or pray in your own words.

"Thank You for Your love and acceptance of me as Your child. I dedicate this time to be with you. Lord, I am listening - I am yours and you are my God. The voice of a stranger and the voice of the enemy I will not hear. Thank You that I have the mind of Christ. I give You permission now, Holy Spirit, to supersede my thinking and speak to me through all of my faculties. I open myself up to You - Father, Son, and Holy Spirit,

Amen."

Worship and Attune

Gratitude and worship (admiration for God and His ways) is the doorway into communion. Allow your mind to settle into thoughts of God, His attributes, His love and kindness toward you. Tell Him inwardly how you feel about Him. Whisper His name and inwardly welcome His presence. Tune in to flowing thoughts, pictures, and feelings. Relax and receive.

Appendix 2: Hearing God's Voice Through Journaling

John 10:27 tells us that God's sheep hear His voice, He knows them, they follow Him, and nothing can pluck them out of His hand. For some, hearing God's voice happens easily and spontaneously and they naturally learn to recognize the still, small voice: hearing God through words or thoughts is their first language. For many others, hearing and discerning the voice of God must be learned and practiced; as the Scriptures teach, God's sheep can and do hear His voice so we can be assured it is God's will to listen for His voice.

While at times God will interrupt our daily activities to speak in a particular moment, it is also wonderful to hear from Him continually, throughout the day because we choose to tune in to His still small voice, as described in 1 Kings 19:11-13. We stay connected to our Father in this way, known as practicing the presence of Christ, or referred to as praying without ceasing (something that would be impossible to do if we were the ones doing all the talking!)

Through the 1 Kings Scripture, we discover what God's voice sounds like most of the time, a "still small voice" or, put another way, spontaneous thoughts that gently come into our minds. That is, God's voice sounds like our thoughts but they are much wiser, more loving, and kinder than our thoughts. They are "thoughts" we have not been thinking and do not involve the intentional use of our own cognitive reasoning: God speaks through our minds but not from our minds. He communes Spirit to spirit and His communication bubbles up from our spirit into our minds as thoughts, so that we can hear His voice, respond to Him, and know Him.

In this book I have provided exercises in the form of questions which will help you to tune in to God's voice. You may also use questions to help with focusing your inner ears to hear God as you commune with Him daily. For example, each morning I begin my day by asking God what He would like to say to me in the course of that day. Then I quiet myself, picture Jesus, and tune in to the inner thoughts and words that begin to flow. I write down what I have sensed God say, then when I am finished listening and writing, I discern and judge if I have heard God by comparing it to God's character, His principles given in the Bible.

Hearing God through journaling His voice is a subject larger than we can address in this book but I pray you are helped by this brief teaching. You, can and probably already do hear His voice.

A wonderful example of hearing God through His still small voice is that of Johannes Brenz a Lutheran reformer, who was warned by an "inner voice" of the approach of the Spanish army at Stuttart. The inner voice instructed him to go to a certain building in the upper city, find an open door, enter it, and hide under the roof. He obeyed, found the door and hid as the voice had instructed. His hiding place was visited by a hen that daily laid two eggs for him until the danger was past. How wonderful it is to hear Gods voice and experience his amazing love, provision, and protection.

Another way God can speak to us through our auditory sense is by music; many hear God through this language, not only through the words of a song but also through the sound of the music, beat, rhythm, and melody. In fact I have had several clear words from God through the songs of birds!

Simple Steps Towards Hearing God's Voice

We may need to "oil the wheels" or "prime the pump" of our inner ears by asking a question; stilling ourselves before God allows us to listen. As we hear His thoughts, it is advisable to write down what we hear so we can read and test what we are hearing after with Scripture and the character of God. You may follow these steps to enable you to hear God's voice.

Repent of any negative words. Pray a simple prayer to

renounce any negative words that may have hindered you from hearing God. Forgive anyone for word curses they have said over you. Receive your forgiveness for sin that may be disturbing your ability to come to God. Repent for wrong use of your hearing (listening to negative or blasphemous words or music). Dedicate your inner ears to God.

Become still. Find a quiet place and come into stillness within by focusing on Jesus Christ. You may wish to whisper His name gently and slowly to settle inwardly.

Picture Jesus. You may ask Holy Spirit where Jesus is in the room with you or picture yourself in a comfortable scene with Him.

Ask a simple, open question. "How do You see me, God?" and "What do You want to say to me about hearing Your voice, seeing You, being with You?" are good starting points. I make it my practice to begin my day with the question "What do You want to say to me today, Lord?"

Keep your question simple and open-ended so that you will not be receiving a yes or no answer. God desires to spend time with you and commune with you. Yes or no answers shorten the conversation; the Lord wants relationship which requires you getting to know His heart for you. There are many questions given in the action steps in this book.

Record your conversation. It is good to keep a journal of your dreams, visions, and God's words to you. Date each conversation or revelatory experience so you can re-read and test them at a later date.

Test what you have heard. When we are learning a new skill, we often benefit from mentors and the advice of more experienced friends. It is a wonderful encouragement and support to have several trusted friends who can help you to discern if you are on track and hearing God.

You can always ask God to give you confirmation on what you are unsure of. I have often been given Scripture verses which, when I then found them in the word, confirmed what God had been speaking to me in my time of listening.

Appendix 3: Testing Revelation

It is important to test the revelation we receive as is stated in scripture[48]. We must not disregard or mike light of Prophecy. Prophecy is God's voice to us directly or through another person, however we need to test and prove that the message is coming from the Spirit of God[49].

There are three possible sources of the spiritual messages we receive. No matter how the message comes to us. The sources are as follows: The Spirit of truth (God), human thinking or desires (human soul), or a lying spirit (demonic spirit). We begin our examination with that which is true and then examine the false then finally our own desires.

The Spirit of Truth or God's Voice

Holy Spirit is the source of revelation; if we listen to His voice, He will show us how to apply it in our day-to-day lives. Therefore, it is imperative that we have invited Him to dwell within our spirits and that we are spending time with Him each day, talking and listening for what He has to say[50]. He will guide us into all truth[51]. As we live in this daily communion with God, we learn to discern the voice of God by the inner peace, or assurance, of Holy Spirit, and can confidently receive guidance and encouragement from Him.

Before we begin to examine revelation, we must be sure to receive Holy Spirit (the Spirit of Truth) by asking Him to cleanse us from all past shortcomings, mistakes, and unforgiveness of the faults of others. This cleansing is made possible because when Jesus died for us, He took all of our past and present faults; He died for all the sin of the world and has risen from the dead. It is the Spirit of Christ that comes to reside within our spirit. We need to renounce all other

---

48 1 Corinthians 14:29 & 1Thessolonians 5:21
49 1 Corinthians 13:8-10
50 Deuteronomy 30:20
51 John 14: 17

commitments and connections to any other god, anti- biblical world view or idol so that we can honestly confess that we have no other gods beside Father, Son, and Holy Spirit. Holy Spirit is the one who can speak to us from within, assure us of truth, and give discernment to know if what we are hearing is our own desires or a lying spirit rather than Him.

God's character and nature: The more we know God, the easier it is to discern His voice. The names given to God are a big clue to His character and nature or ways. Following is a list of names for the Father, Son, and Holy Spirit found in the Bible (this is not a complete list of the names of God, but will be of some help).

God the Father

Almighty, Fortress, Healer, Heavenly Father, Holy One, I AM, Judge, King of Kings, The Lord is there, Lord of Lords, God is Love, Mighty God, Most High, My Banner, My Glory and the Lifter of my head, My Peace, My Righteousness

God the Son

Lord Jesus Christ, Advocate, Almighty, Author and Finisher of our faith, Bread of Life, Captain of Salvation, Cornerstone, Creator, Day Spring, Deliverer, Desire of the Nations, The Door, Good Shepherd, Immanuel (God with us), King of kings, Lamb of God, Life, Light of the World, The Vine, The Truth, The Way

God the Holy Spirit

Comforter, Counsel, Fear of the Lord, Knowledge of God, Might, Our Guide, Peace, Spirit of Christ, Spirit of Holiness, Spirit of Truth and of Wisdom, Understanding

We test the revelation by comparing it with the character and nature of the names of God. For example, if the revelation is in agreement with God's names, with His nature and character, we know it is from Him.

Lying or Deceitful Spirits, The Enemy's Voice[52]

We can discern the negative voice of the enemy fairly easily because it aligns with the names, nature, and fruit of our enemy. Listed below are some examples to assist you.

Names: The enemy of God, The Devil, Satan, Deceiver, Father of Lies, Serpent, Accuser, Murderer, Thief, Robber, and a fallen angle of light. Nature: the enemy is prideful, boastful, arrogant, rude, selfish, unkind, greedy, and egotistical.

Fruit: Enemy revelation produces: sin, fear, disunity, depression, rage, low self-worth, pride, and loss of many kinds.

Aligning Revelation With Scripture

Scripture is our guide for confirmation; when we compare the revelation with Scripture, the Holy Spirit will reveal if it is compatible and in agreement with what God has already said. If the revelation you have received does not align with, or contradicts, what God has already said in the Bible, it is probably not God speaking.

There is an example of this in the Bible: Balaam the prophet[53] accepted money to curse Israel, despite God's previous command not to curse Israel. Because Balaam listened to the nation paying him to curse Israel, God intervened and set him straight through the words of a donkey. This drastic example would not have been necessary, however, if Balaam had used discernment to align the request of the enemy of Israel with God's nature (God is Love[54], the one who blesses His people)[55] and what God had already spoken about blessing Israel. While Balaam did not have written scripture in his day, we do and can therefore use Scripture as a reference for what God has already said, and to learn about His character.

---

52   Jeremiah 23:13
53   Numbers 22:15-35
54   Deuteronomy 7:9; Psalm 36:7; Psalm 42:8; Joel 2:13; Jonah 4:2; Romans 8:39;   1John 2:5; 1John 3:1:-10; 1 John 4:6-8
55   Psalm 98:3; Romans 12:14

Testing Revelation By the Fruit or Results

At times, we can anticipate the outcome of an action or direction before we take it. We can, for example, tell whether it will lead to: loving God; loving our neighbour; bringing blessing, unity, or division among people; blessing and love, or away from love and blessing. At other times we will not fully realize the fruit or results till we have stepped out and the action actually comes to pass. We need wisdom and sensitivity to Holy Spirit to discern. We will eventually see and understand the results if the revelation brings positive outcomes. Actions resulting from godly revelation will increase the fruit of the spirit in our lives and the lives of those with whom we interact[56].

How to Discern Our Inner Thoughts From God's Voice

Our cognitive, rational mind works to make decisions and think, or ponder, by our active choice. When we want to hear from God about a choice or decision in our lives, we can sometimes allow our own feelings and desires to interfere with hearing God. In order to distinguish our own inner voice from that of God's we first need to submit our will to God; we are to position ourselves to accept His answer regardless of whether it is what we desire in a particular situation. As we spend more time with God, we learn to distinguish between our own thoughts and preferences, and God's voice.

It is essential that we do not hold our own desires or opinions higher than God's will. We will not be able to hear or discern God's voice clearly if we are very passionate about receiving a certain answer: we will always hear what we want to hear if we have very strong feelings on a subject. In such a situation the answer we desire becomes too important and blocks God's answer.

In the example of the prophet Balaam[57], when he initially asked

---

56   See Galatians 5:21-23 for a list of the fruit of the Spirit
57   Numbers 22-24

God about the offer of money to curse Israel, he received an answer which was certainly in line with God's character (God loves, blesses and favours His people). Because Balaam wanted in his heart to accept the money, he decided to check again, and this time heard the answer he wanted to hear; the money changed Balaam's ability to discern clearly because his desire for money was stronger than his desire for God's will.

We need to be able to receive any answer God gives so we must take the time to move from a strong desire to fulfill our will and become neutral. By purposing to become neutral about decisions, we will accept God's divine choice, only then will we be positioned to hear clearly from God. As we spend more time listening and talking with God, we learn his character. Knowledge of the character of God (His desire is to give us abundant life, that He will not with hold any good thing from us) helps to motivate us toward accepting His good perfect and pleasing will. I have often had to wait to ask God about a decision or for His will on a topic till my desire is submitted to God's answer whatever it may be. It often takes time and prayer to be ready (in neutral mode) to hear what God wants and not to just hear what I want. The wait is always well worth it.

The Counsel of Others: Another safe guard when discerning God's voice is to share your revelation with some trusted friends. We find safety in the counsel of many. I have several close and trusted friends who hear God well and when I am in need of advice I know they will take time to go over what I feel God has revealed to me. I have done the same for others to bring reassurance and discernment. It is a blessing to find counsel with those who love God, are growing in their friendship with Him, and value listening to His voice.

Conformation from God: Just as a loving father will carefully instruct and guide us, God in His great patience and kindness will make sure we understand His communication to us. As we learn to discern the voice of God, God confirms what He wants us to know. When we are not receiving or perhaps not understanding His message He will show us in other ways.

For example: God may confirm an inner-knowing that we need to give a financial gift through a dream, journaling of His voice a scripture or a prophetic word. Keep in mind that if we have no means to give it might not be a message from God. I had such an example. I felt I heard God tell me to give a friend some money, at the time I was in a prayer meeting after which I was to buy the families groceries. I had the sense to give to her then toward end of the meeting she asked for prayer for a financial need. She did not state the amount needed but I had my conformation. I had just enough money for our family's needs however I felt convicted to give my friend the money which turned out to be the exact amount she needed. I continued on to the grocery store with what money I had left and was greeted at the door by another friend who gave me the exact amount I had given away, he had felt to repay money that I didn't even remember loaning him. God works in wonderful ways to confirm the promptings of His Voice

Thank You

It is my prayer that you have found this book helpful in your friendship with God. I would love to hear from you and it would be most helpful to have feedback. I encourage you to write a review to help other readers decide on this book.

Other Books

Divine Focus
Living in Union with God

Arranged as a trilogy, Divine Focus explores the subject of practicing the presence of Christ. It explains how humans may live in complete agreement with Father, Son and Holy Spirit. Communion with God moment by moment is modeled beautifully by our Jesus Christ, so each of the sections of this trilogy are named after His self-description.

Section 1: **"The Life"** examines Jesus Christ as our example and teacher on the subject of living in perfect focus.

Section 2: **"The Truth"** contains essays on truths which explain the path and process of being tuned to the presence of God.

Section 3: **"The Way"** details disciplines and practices which Christians through the ages have used to connect in intimate friendship with God.

Listen Up!
Discerning the voice of God for your everyday life.

Jesus said, "My sheep know My voice" – and you can tune in and hear from God every day. You will find in this little book practical and easy-to-understand keys for unlocking the door to knowing God's voice. As you read and work through the listening prayer exercises, you will find the pleasure of knowing the One who made you. God has a beautiful plan for your life and you can discover His voice, take His lead, and follow the path Jesus has marked out for you.

Chapters include:
- Hearing With More Than Ears: The Ways God Speaks
- The Faith Factor: The Key That Unlocks Supernatural Life

- Stop Look & Listen: Journaling Your Conversations With God
- Discerning Direction: Knowing What the Signs Say
- Christian Meditation: Using The Grey Matter and More
- Checking It Out: God? Satan? Or Just Wishful Thinking?
- How Others Have Learned to Listen Up

The Restoration Manual

A Guide to Restoring the Soul Through Inner-Healing

Developed from Biblical techniques, this approach to prayer counselling is used for Inner Healing of the personality or soul. It is a practical tool to enable every Christian to pray through areas of blockage and emotional pain. Once learned, this method can be used in subsequent areas of emotional pain and blockages to continue on the road of healing and restoration using a free workbook download.

Chapter Headings:

- The Wounded Soul
- Seven Steps for Restoring the Soul
- Restoring Generational Lines
- Correcting Soul Ties
- Healing Painful Memories
- Renouncing Negative Words
- Renewing Truth and Purpose
- Cleansing from the Demonic
- Living by Holy Spirit's Power
- Aftercare
- Leaders Tools

The Kingdom Within

Knowing God the Spirit and learning to flow in and through Him.

This book is for people looking for a primer on Holy Spirit (Holy Spirit 101). It will help you to learn about His nature, graces and gifts but even more importantly it is designed to draw you into a deeper friendship with God. It provides practical and easy ways for you to tune your heart to Him. Each chapter has suggested meditation questions which are designed to enable you to understand what God has for you.

Chapters include:

- Coming to Know the Holy Spirit ~ Progressing Toward Union With God
- Knowing Holy Spirit ~ His Name, Symbolic Descriptions, The Sevenfold Spirit
- Holy Spirit the Giver ~ Fruit of the Spirit, Gifts of the Spirit
- Positioned to Receive ~ Focus, Faith, Filled With the Spirit
- Revealer of Truth ~ How God Speaks, Our Spiritual Senses
- Spiritual Disciplines ~ Listening Prayer, Meditation, Fasting, Spiritual Retreat
- Testing Revelation
- Ministering through the Spirit ~ Praying Like Jesus, Releasing the Flow
- Teamwork ~ Prophetic Etiquette, Seeking God Together

The Language of Dreams and Visions

A Handbook for Interpretation and Symbolism.

This handbook is a guide to understanding and interpreting dreams and visions. It contains an extensive and valuable dictionary of biblical and cultural symbols giving insight into

God's way of communication. It includes a template dream journal for recording and interpreting dreams.

Chapters include:

- God Is Speaking
- Supernatural Encounters
- Defining Dream and Vision
- Restoring Dream and Visionary Capacities
- Soaking or Listening Prayer
- Dream and Vision Recording
- Interpretation
- Testing Revelation
- Dictionary of Symbols
- Biblical Reference Section for Dreams, Visions and Bible References for the Names of God

About Yvonne

Rev. Yvonne Prentice,

Pastor at His Presence Ministries

Credentialed with ECCiC

Once a native of Australia, Yvonne lives and works in Canada. She has been married to her husband Bob for more than 45 years. They have five grown children and eight adorable grandchildren. Yvonne has been a friend of God for over 40 years and is growing to love Him more each year. Under God's direction and anointing Yvonne produces:

- Customized prayer blankets

- Scripture meditation CD's

- Manuals & books on topics such as inner-healing, listening prayer, meditation, interpreting dreams and visions, knowing the Holy Spirit, and discerning destiny

Yvonne brings encouragement and hope to many. She loves to introduce others to the practice of "soaking" or listening prayer, and Biblical meditation. She loves to foster times in God's presence helping others deepen their friendship with Jesus Christ. Regularly ministering at retreats and workshops, Yvonne's heart is to see God's people grow in intimacy with Jesus Christ by practicing His presence daily.

Contact

Email: hispresenceministries@gmail.com

Facebook: through her page His Presence Ministries.

Blog: pushingtheedges.blogspot.com

www.ingramcontent.com/pod-product-compliance
Lightning Source LLC
Chambersburg PA
CBHW072006060426
42446CB00042B/2000